MOZART

a biography by David Sachs

New York   London   Tokyo

Copyright © Quick Fox, 1979

All rights reserved.

Printed in the United States of America.

International Standard Book Number: 0-8256-3159-9
Library of Congress Catalog Card Number: 79-65943

No part of this book may be reproduced or transmitted in any form or by any means, electronic or mechanical, including photocopying, without permission in writing from the publisher: Quick Fox, 33 West 60th Street, New York 10023.

In Great Britain: Book Sales Ltd., 78 Newman Street, London W1P 3LA.

In Canada: Gage Trade Publishing, P.O. Box 5000, 164 Commander Blvd., Agincourt, Ontario M1S 3C7.

In Japan: Quick Fox, 4-26-22 Jingumae, Shibuya-ku, Tokyo 150.

Designed by Kay Susmann

Cover illustration by Sandy Hoffman

MOZART

For Noah

The annual Mostly Mozart festival at Lincoln Center in New York.

Contents

	Introduction: Heavy into Mozart	11
Part One:	The Child Is Father of the Man	
	1. A Star Is Born	15
	2. Life on the Road	28
	3. Down and Out	47
Part Two:	The Last Golden Decade	
	4. Set Me Free	63
	5. What Price Glory?	79
	6. Midnight Sun	96
	Recommended Records	117
	Index of Works	119

A two-year-old Mozart admirer.

Introduction

Heavy into Mozart

I grew up loving rock music; Chuck Berry was my first favorite composer (though I didn't think of him as such). Music had the power to take me outside the everyday and inside myself.

The first piece of classical music I really heard—that is, heard and understood and loved—was by Mozart. A friend was playing a record, and I remember thinking that the music was like nothing I had ever heard: strong, compellingly beautiful. It was the overture to *Don Giovanni*. When the overture ended a man started to sing. I liked to hear people sing but I certainly did not like opera. Yet I kept on listening because the music sounded so alive. I recognized that this was classical music, which I associated with dullness and deadness; but this music was both fresh and exciting. As I listened I realized that some of the melodies and harmonies were not unrelated to much rock I knew, although the total impact was completely new.

That same day I bought a recording of *Don Giovanni,* the first classical music I ever purchased. There were four records in a box. I played side 1 (the side with the overture) again and again. It sounded so good, and there was so much new to hear each time, that I was reluctant to play side 2; I didn't want to be disappointed. Of course curiosity won out, and side 2 sounded even better. I played it again and again, then sides 1 and 2 consecutively, over and over. By then I wanted to know what everyone was singing about, so I followed the libretto: the story proved intriguing. At last I listened to the entire opera straight through, with continuously increasing amazement.

After much time with *Don Giovanni* I wanted to hear more Mozart; there turned out to be plenty. Each new work I heard revealed new wonders, gave me new pleasures. I began listening to music all the time. It changed my life.

New favorite composers emerged—Bach, Debussy, Mahler—but a special feeling for Mozart remained. The more Mozart's music meant to me, the more interested I became in the man who composed it; how he lived, his time and place. Mozart is surrounded by a legend—a name carved in stone, a plaster head, a big gun in the arsenal of culture snobbery—which has little to do with the real man who created such glorious and accessible music.

The Mozart bibliography is vast and unendingly rich. I have relied on two exceptional feats of scholarship: Emily Anderson's translation and edition of *The Letters of Mozart and His Family* (St. Martin's Press, 1966) and Otto Deutsch's *Mozart: A Documentary Biography* (Stanford University Press, 1965). Together, these primary sources provide a comprehensive portrait of Mozart in his own words and those of his father, sister, wife, and numerous contemporaries. Among many excellent biographies I am especially indebted to two outstanding ones: Eric Blom's *Mozart* (Collier Books, 1962) and Alfred Einstein's *Mozart: His Character, His Work* (Oxford University Press, 1945). It is a pleasure to acknowledge Jeanette Mall, most responsive of editors, Margaret Wolf, most skilled of copyeditors, and Kim Dramer-Pannell, most resourceful of photo researchers.

Since music expresses what words cannot, writing about a composer leaves much unsaid. Details of Mozart's life illuminate his music but do not account for it. In every sense the music speaks for itself.

— David Sachs
August, 1979

I

The Child Is Father of the Man

1.

A Star Is Born

Great geniuses have the shortest biographies.
— Emerson

No one knows what a genius is, but everyone can see that certain men and women live special lives, lives that are important to millions of people across the barriers of time and space. Their lives have impact: in a way geniuses even cheat death, because who they were and what they did continue to matter after they die.

However startling their ability, geniuses are human beings, sharing the same needs, desires, and concerns as everyone else. They create and they try to earn a living; they produce and they try to find happiness. Their lives combine the exceptional and the ordinary, the unique and the common. They have an urge to express the widest range of experience in its full complexity and richness. At the center of their lives burns a powerful love.

A musical genius, as great as there has been, was born at eight o'clock in the evening on January 27, 1756, in Salzburg, Austria. The odds against his surviving were good: most babies in eighteenth-century Europe died in their first year. Five of his own brothers and sisters had died in infancy, leaving one four-year-old sister. The boy was christened Johann Chrysostom Wolfgang Theophilus Mozart, an impressive-sounding name full of meaning. January 27 is the nameday of Saint John Chrysostom, the patron saint of preachers; his name means "golden mouth," which suggests sweet songs. Wolfgang is the name of a local saint and his maternal grandfather. Theophilus, "God lover," was first Germanized to Gottlieb and then Latinized to Amadeus. By the time he was ten the world knew him as Wolfgang Amadeus Mozart; to his family, he was Wolferl.

Today Salzburg is a resort city of one hundred thousand people which Mozart made famous posthumously. It is the home of the Mozart industry: the annual music festival, the Mozarteum (a combination music school, concert hall, and ar-

Salzburg.

chives), various Mozart residences, souvenirs of all kinds. In 1756, Salzburg was a town of ten thousand, a fortress by a river in the foothills of the Alps. Princes had filled the town with so many Italian-style churches that it became known as the "German Rome." The combination of architecture and landscape led the naturalist Alexander Humboldt to describe it as one of the three most beautiful towns in the world.

There was another side of Salzburg. It was provincial and somewhat backward. In popular German plays of the time, the boob talked in Salzburg dialect; the population had a reputation for crudeness and low humor.

Salzburg was the capital of a small state of the same name, in theory independent. It was one of the forty German states of the so-called Holy Roman Empire, a loose conglomeration of countries from Hungary to the Netherlands and from Italy to Denmark. In 1756, Voltaire wrote that it was "neither holy, Roman, nor an empire"; in reality it was an extension of Austria.

Each state had its own currency, tariffs, and government. Salzburg's ruler was a prince and archbishop, holding both secular and religious power. Each prince-archbishop was elected by a small group of wealthy landowners.

Like the other states, Salzburg had a court and nobility, modeled as closely as possible on Louis XIV's Versailles. Each court spent lavishly on parties, hunts, and other entertainments, including musical ones. The court was a dream world of fantasies amid the realities of war and starvation. Most people were serfs, tied to the land much as they were in the Middle Ages. The contrasts were striking.

The year Mozart was born, the bloodiest war yet fought, the Seven Years' War, began. Two wars in one—England against France and Prussia against Austria—it involved almost every European nation. It was fought on three continents: Europe, North America (the French and Indian War), and India (1756 was the year of the Black Hole of Calcutta). It was the dying days of feudalism, the world of lord and peasants; not a very pretty time for the vast majority of Europeans.

Wolfgang was born into a musical family, a fact which completely shaped his life. His father, Leopold Mozart, was a composer and a musician of some renown. He was born in Augsburg, just across the Salzburg border, in Bavaria, the son of a bookbinder and a free citizen (neither aristocrat nor peasant). As a young man Leopold sang and played organ, but he was not exceptional. He went to Salzburg to attend the Benedictine university, first to become a priest (he was always a devout Catholic), later to study law. But for unknown reasons Leopold was expelled from school and was soon working as a violinist for Count Thurn und Taxis, whose family held the postal monopoly in central Europe. His first compositions were published in 1740, and by 1743 he was playing and composing for Salzburg's prince, Archbishop Schrattenbach.

Leopold Mozart wrote music in all the standard forms of the period, basically three: church music (masses and hymns), theater music, and chamber music (including orchestral works). Like most music composed in his or any other time, Leopold Mozart's works have not lasted. They were not special. His greatest success was a manual on how to play the violin, called *The Violin School*. It was published, favorably reviewed, reprinted, and translated; it was a standard text for more than a

Leopold Mozart.

The house where Wolfgang was born.

hundred years. He finished it in 1756, which was the year Wolfgang was born.

Leopold married Maria Anna Pertl in 1747. Born in 1720, she was the daughter of a local tax collector (Wolfgang's namesake) who was also a singer and choirmaster. Although not a musician, she loved music and was sympathetic to the difficulties a musician had in making a living. Her letters show a cheerful, warm-hearted, not particularly strong-willed woman. She was beautiful; at the time of her marriage she and Leopold were called the handsomest couple in Salzburg.

The Mozarts were not poor, least of all by eighteenth-century standards. They rented spacious rooms in the center of town, and they employed at least one maid and a cook. A middle-class family, they were part of the small but growing urban population of traders and artisans that wound up dominating Europe and the world a century later.

The small but real chances of material advancement were always in the front of Leopold Mozart's mind. His obsession with money and success was rooted in the insecurity of middle-class life, which existed in the huge gap between the peasants' extreme poverty and the gentry's enormous wealth. He was upwardly mobile in the most strenuous way, intent on entering the ranks of the privileged.

The only route that Leopold could take was music. He began teaching his daughter, Maria Anna (called Nannerl), to play the harpsichord as soon as she could talk. Child prodigies were proving extremely profitable, and Nannerl's great aptitude for the harpsichord filled her father's head with ideas. Perhaps she could play for the aristocracy, become rich and famous, and of course spread his fame as a teacher. Nannerl practiced every day.

Wolfgang literally grew up with the sound of music ringing in his ears, and no one was surpised when the three-year-old boy sat down at the harpsichord and began to pick out notes. What was surprising was that he began at once to find combinations of notes—chords—that pleased him, and that he remembered and repeated. His favorites were thirds (for example, C and E) and sixths (C and A).

All Wolfgang's gifts emerged spontaneously, at play. He was just enjoying himself, playing for the pleasure that it gave him. By the time he was four he could perform short pieces from memory without mistakes; by five he was inventing his own little pieces, mostly minuets, which his father copied down in a notebook he kept for his son. His mind was full of wonder as he wrote—and of the possibilities the boy offered to the family's fortune.

Nannerl remembered years later that Wolfgang was never forced to play or compose. On the contrary, he had to be stopped from playing day and night. "As long as the piece of music lasted, he was all music himself."

Leopold Mozart had few personal friends. He was suspicious and aloof, inclined to believe the worst of people. "Accept it as a universal truth that all men tell lies," he wrote. One of the few people to be a guest in his home was Johann Schachtner, the Salzburg court trumpeter. When he recalled Wolfgang's childhood, Schachtner remembered when he and Leopold found Wolfgang, then four, busy with pen and music paper. Each time Wolfgang wrote, he dipped the pen in the ink bottle, splattering blobs of ink, which he smeared with his palm. Surveying the mess, Leopold asked Wolfgang what he was doing. "I'm writing a harpsichord concerto; it'll be done soon." Leopold took the paper and laughed, but gradually made out the notes underneath the smeared ink. There was a melody. "It looks difficult," Leopold commented. "That's why it's a concerto," answered Wolfgang, who rushed to the harpsichord and began to play his creation. He made lots of mistakes, Schachtner recalled, but it was still a four-year-old playing music which he had written. The two adults sat down and cooled off.

From the second he realized the extent of Wolfgang's musical ability, Leopold Mozart devoted himself to his son's musical development. His entire life revolved around Wolfgang; Leopold lived for him and through him. He was his son's constant companion, his greatest influence, his only teacher. He spent as much of each day with the boy as he could, his job notwithstanding. He was determined that under his supervision Wolfgang would become a great—the world's greatest—composer. Leopold started at once, providing an in-depth course in music theory with hours of practice. As the eighteenth-century British music historian Charles Burney (who later heard Mozart play) wrote, Wolfgang had "every advantage of situation and culture joined to the profusion of natural endowments."

Leopold's ambitions were limitless. He sincerely believed that Wolfgang's talent was a gift from God (it certainly seemed to be a "gift," and it had to come from someplace), and that God had chosen to honor Leopold through his son. By this time Leopold probably realized that his own musical gifts were second-rate; in Wolfgang he saw a path to perfection. Leopold Mozart was cynical about the world, uncharitable to his fellow human beings, bigoted and authoritarian. He ran his small household like that of a prince, looking after every silly detail personally and seriously. But when his children were involved he was tireless, responsive, and fair, and he inspired the deepest devotion in them both, especially Wolfgang. "After God, Papa," the boy would say, and mean it.

People who knew Mozart as a child remembered an extremely, maybe even neurotically affectionate boy. Schachtner recalled that Wolfgang would ask his parents and their friends if they loved him, sometimes repeating the question many times a day. When one of them would teasingly answer no, he would burst into tears. He was obedient to the point of submissiveness. Though obviously cared for, encouraged, and treated kindly—he was never beaten, unlike most boys at that time—Wolfgang couldn't be reassured often enough that he was loved. He couldn't stop asking.

Perhaps this childhood need to give and receive affection found a place in Mozart's music. Music is abstract, and it is not easy to determine what it means, what it is about. But people have always known that music was about something; from its beginnings as song and clapping, music related to people's emotions. It was only music when it had a human effect.

Every night Wolfgang stood on a chair and sang a duet, in nonsense Italian, with his father. Then he kissed Leopold on the tip of his nose and promised to keep him in a glass box when he grew old, to protect him from the wind. Wolfgang had a core of genuine sweetness, felt by everybody who knew him. After his death this quality was exaggerated to ludicrous dimensions, producing an image of Mozart as sugary as marzipan, a Dresden doll, a perpetual child in a powdered wig. But as Schachtner recalled, "he might have become the most wicked villain, so susceptible was he to every attraction." Angel and devil, musician and little boy: Mozart's life was full of opposites.

Except for a brief appearance as a choirboy when he was five, Wolfgang was kept out of the public eye. Only a handful of Leopold's cronies knew about Wolfgang's unusual talents. Leopold, who liked to assume the worst, feared Wolfgang would inspire jealousy and disbelief. The boy had to live up to the highest expectations. Leopold relentlessly stressed the need to practice diligently, to concentrate completely, to remember flawlessly: in a word, perfection. Nothing less satisfied this severe and demanding teacher, this father.

As a young boy Wolfgang was afraid of the trumpet, and Leopold decided to cure him—with a technique familiar to anyone who has learned to swim by being thrown in the water. Schachtner agreed to sneak up behind him and blow loud and long. When he did he immediately regretted it; Wolfgang screamed his head off. Eventually Wolfgang overcame his dislike and used trumpets and trombones most effectively.

Another trait stood out in the boy and stayed with him throughout his life. He was always in motion: his hands swirling, his feet beating time on the floor. No doubt Wolfgang would today be diagnosed hyperactive.

By the time Wolfgang was six, his musical talent and knowledge were so advanced that Leopold decided he was ready to be exhibited to the world. So was Nannerl; her abilities were impressive, and at eleven she was still a child prodigy. If Leopold delayed, she would reach puberty, and then she'd be less of an attraction. Leopold Mozart thought of everything.

Nannerl Mozart lived most of her life in the shadow of her brother. She played the harpsichord brilliantly, and she could compose too, primarily songs. But she did not become a composer. Perhaps Leopold never encouraged her creative efforts; maybe he told her to stick to the written notes when she wanted to improvise. He more than likely shared the widespread belief that women by definition could not compose. Or she may just not have had sufficient talent. No one can ever know.

In January 1762, the Mozart family left for Munich, the capital of Bavaria, seventy miles northwest of Salzburg. It was a dress rehearsal, a tryout for future tours that Leopold was already planning. Wolfgang and Nannerl played at the court of the elector of Bavaria, their first time before an audience. After three weeks they returned home, having passed the test without a hitch: no stage fright, no memory lapses. The proud papa was just beginning: the next stop was Vienna, the imperial Austrian capital.

Leopold Mozart needed time to plan, promote, and supervise his children's tours. He got it by sacrificing any chance for his own professional success. He watched a series of less-talented musicians become Salzburg music director while he remained an assistant. He had only one full-time job: Wolfgang. Leopold was convinced that it was God's will to put his son's interests (as he understood them) first.

Maria Theresa, empress of Austria.

An allegro composed by the six-year-old Wolfgang.

In return, he exercised complete control over the boy. Wolfgang never went to school, never had friends his own age, never had time to himself. Leopold continued in command long after Wolfgang grew up; he gave up his control reluctantly and bitterly.

The summer of 1762 was an exciting one for the Mozarts. It was hot elsewhere too. In St. Petersburg, early in the morning of July 9, Catherine the Great was proclaimed empress of Russia following a coup led by her then current lover.

Vienna, then the greatest city of central Europe, had a population of two hundred thousand and an active cultural, especially musical, scene. Opera, theater, and all kinds of amusements prospered despite the war. As the center of a multinational empire, Vienna was a cosmopolitan city; native Hungarians, Czechs, Italians, Slavs, and Germans mingled with a continuous flow of other Europeans. The imperial palace, Schönbrunn, was second only to Versailles in grandeur, pomp, and waste.

The four Mozarts left for Vienna in September. Wolfgang began performing on the road; his first public performance was at an inn. Later they stopped at a monastery, and Wolfgang saw an organ for the first time. He played at once, and the monks "left their eating and ran to hear, open-mouthed with astonishment," Leopold wrote. At the gates of Vienna, Wolfgang charmed the customs officer by "playing him a minuet on his little fiddle." The family got through customs quickly and toll free.

News of the children had already reached the court, and they were invited to perform at Schönbrunn. Empress Maria Theresa and her husband were both amateur musicians; their daughters were reported to "sing well, for princesses." The

Wolfgang, age 6.

royal family was delighted. The emperor called Wolfgang a little magician, not the most thoughtful comment he could have made to a boy already so serious about music. On his way to the harpsichord, Wolfgang slipped on the highly polished floor. One of the princesses, then seven years old, helped him up. He told her he would marry her when he grew up, out of gratitude. Better for her if he had; instead, Marie Antoinette married the king of France and was guillotined in 1793, shortly after Mozart's death.

Wolfgang demonstrated his affectionate nature by jumping up onto Maria Theresa's lap and kissing her vigorously, no doubt quite a surprise for her majesty. She was lavish in return. In exchange for providing the entertainment, Leopold Mozart was allowed to see the inside of the palace and was given some money and dress clothes for his kids—imperial hand-me-downs, hers pink and silver, his lavender and gold. Leopold spent some of the money having the children's portrait painted in their new clothes.

After their success at the palace, the children were taken up by the nobility, eager to copy the imperial family's model. Wolfgang and Nannerl played in the best homes in Vienna; as one count wrote, "the poor little fellow plays marvelously." The spectacle was amusing, but to Leopold's dismay, hard cash was seldom forthcoming in interesting amounts.

In the midst of these appearances, Wolfgang came down with scarlet fever. He had been sick before and was often sick again. It is possible that all the moving around weakened him and permanently damaged his health. It is also possible that

Nannerl Mozart, age 11.

he would have contracted the same diseases in his unsanitary Salzburg home, where five babies had died. He recovered quickly and continued to perform. Despite his sickness he had plenty of energy. He needed it.

The family returned home in January 1763. Leopold Mozart was more confident than ever; both children had amazed all hearers. Now the sky was the limit: a grand tour of Europe, as far as Paris and maybe even London.

In February, the Peace of Paris ended the Seven Years' War. In its most savage battle more than thirty thousand soldiers died in one afternoon. Great Britain gained complete control of eastern North America and the Indian subcontinent.

Wolfgang and Nannerl practiced every day. In addition to his keyboard mastery, Wolfgang became a whiz on the violin, his father's instrument. According to Schachtner, Wolfgang taught himself; his ear was accurate to an eighth-tone.

Leopold Mozart could not doubt that his prodigies—the word also means monsters—would be acclaimed wherever they went. The future depended on being recognized by some royal music lover, whose patronage would provide both money and the opportunity to compose. Somewhere in Europe Leopold would find the right one.

On June 9, 1763, they left Salzburg once again.

2.

Life on the Road

I am still alive and always merry as usual.
—Mozart, 1770

The grand tour of Europe lasted three and a half years, and it set a pattern: Wolfgang Amadeus Mozart spent fifteen of his thirty-five years on the road.

In terms of money and fame, the grand tour was the high point of Wolfgang's life. He and Nannerl and Leopold were celebrities across the continent; wrote one contemporary, "nobody in all Europe is as famous as Herr Mozart with his two children."

The family traveled by coach, occasionally taking short ferry rides. The roads were bad and dangerous, and expensive to travel because of the numberless custom houses in what later became Germany. Munich, Augsburg, Heidelberg, Cologne—at every town the children performed. On sight, Wolfgang learned to play a pedal organ, standing up so his feet could reach the pedals. "What many achieve after much labor comes to him as a new gift of God," Leopold wrote.

A concert in Frankfurt gives a good idea of the kind of show Leopold put on. It combined music and spectacle, serious art and flashy tricks. Something for everyone: part concert, part freak show.

It was a family act. First Nannerl appeared. Long and difficult harpsichord pieces were her specialty, and she played them with "astonishing precision." Then her brother, dressed in his finest suit, took over. He played popular tunes on both a small spinet and a violin. (He carried travel-sized models of the two instruments.) At the keyboard he played original pieces, arrangements of and variations on other works, and requests from the audience. For a change of pace he played a long violin piece. He then played his spinet while the keyboard was covered with a cloth, and he identified pitches, singly and in chords, played on any instrument, including bells, drinking glasses, and clocks. He ended by improvising on keyboard or organ for as long as people cared to listen.

Wolfgang's spinet.

Johann Wolfgang Goethe, soon to emerge as Germany's leading poet, saw one of these Frankfurt concerts when he was fourteen. Years later he recalled "the little man with the wig and the sword." One of the first Mozart enthusiasts, Goethe wished Mozart had lived long enough to set *Faust* to music. "A phenomenon like that of Mozart remains inexplicable," he wrote in his old age.

Wolfgang had the temperament to match his talent. In some ways he was like any child star: cute and spoiled. He was important and he knew it. Leopold wrote to friends that he was always happy and high-spirited, occasionally "naughty," and completely absorbed in music. From the beginning, Wolfgang hated any joking around about music. Loud, harsh, or wrong notes made him angry and tearful. His personality became as sensitive as his ear.

He was imaginative, as his playing suggested. Nannerl remembered her brother had invented a "magic kingdom of Back," in which he was the king. Long hours on the road were spent making up names for its cities and towns. Nannerl didn't remember what the name meant—maybe as they kept pushing farther and farther, part of Wolfgang wanted "back."

One morning Wolfgang woke up crying. He told Leopold he missed his neighbors in Salzburg. He was a seven-year-old boy with no friends, far from home.

Economically, Leopold Mozart was at the mercy of local princes and gentry, not famous for their generosity. Wealth was still in the hands of serf-owning lords of the manor, most of whom were as indifferent to other people's needs as they were blind to the fact that their own days were numbered. Frederick the Great's sister "showered Wolferl with kisses . . . but she herself has no money, and neither the

Voltaire.

innkeeper nor the postmaster are paid in kisses," wrote the practical father. The gentry preferred trinkets to cash as payment for music; "with all the snuff boxes and leather cases and such we could open a shop."

In November, the Mozarts arrived in Paris, the cultural capital of Europe. Twice as populous as Vienna, Paris was also the intellectual heart of the western world. The great figures of the Enlightenment were all alive and active. Voltaire, in exile in Geneva, was at the height of his fame, leading the attack on the feudal institutions of state and church. Three years before he had published *Candide,* satirizing the complacency he saw around him: "If this is the best of all possible worlds, what then are the others?" Rousseau had just written *The Social Contract*; its first sentence is as revolutionary today as it was in 1763: "Man is born free and everywhere he is in chains." Paris was full of new ideas: romanticism, back to nature, free thinking.

While the majority of Parisians struggled to earn enough to eat and live in the rapidly growing slums, the aristocracy indulged itself lavishly. Leopold took his family to the opera, which in France was called "lyric tragedy." These operas were four-hour spectacles, loosely based on classical mythology, with interspersed ballets, choruses, elaborate scenery, and the most dazzling special effects money could buy. For the first time Wolfgang saw music captivate an audience of thousands.

Wolfgang, too, was captivating. After one public concert, he and Nannerl were invited to play at Versailles. There they met King Louis XV and his mistress, Madame de Pompadour. Wolfgang, affectionate as ever, tried to kiss her, too; she

Rousseau.

repulsed him. "Who does she think she is?" the boy asked. His successes had begun to go to his head.

The children delighted their hosts with their playing, Wolfgang again guessing pitches and improvising to everyone's amazement. He played difficult pieces upon sight and composed his own. Two sonatas for harpsichord and violin, "by J.G. Wolfgang Mozart of Salzburg, aged seven," were dedicated to the king's daughter by "your very humble, very obedient, and very small servant." Leopold paid to have these sonatas engraved as his son's opus 1. They are skillful imitations of the prevailing style, remarkable only because they were written by a child, and because the child became Mozart.

The style that Mozart wrote in was called "galant," inspired by the pretty, empty court life of the time. Its main concerns were lightness, simplicity, charm, and decoration. It was music meant to be played in the fantasy world of formal gardens and drawing rooms, Disneylands in the middle of starving peasants and urban poor.

The musical taste of Europe had changed dramatically between 1720 and 1750. Baroque music, massive and complex, went so completely out of fashion that Mozart, born just six years after Bach died, didn't hear a note of Bach's music until 1782. It was as if the great baroque composers had never lived. Bach's *Brandenburg* Concertos were sold as scrap paper; his sonatas for solo violin were found in a butter store, about to be wrapping paper. Half of Bach's instrumental music disappeared for good. Europeans didn't hear a major Bach work until 1829, when Mendelssohn conducted the *Saint Matthew Passion*. (Imagine a composer in 1900 who hadn't

Leopold, Wolfgang, and Nannerl Mozart: Paris, 1764.

heard any Brahms or Wagner.) Today, with few exceptions, most galant music of the 1750s and 1760s is seldom heard.

The Mozarts spent five months in Paris, and they were the talk of the town. Leopold had a triple portrait painted in oils: he is playing the violin, Wolfgang is at the harpsichord, and Nannerl seems to be singing. Nannerl is good-looking in an unusual way—Wolfgang called her "Horseface"—and her brother looks intense yet angelic. Leopold had hundreds of copies engraved, which he sold at every concert, like the professors selling pictures of Lola Lola in the film *The Blue Angel*. The Parisian success increased Leopold's already hearty appetite; overcoming his dislike of sea voyages, he took his family across the English channel, arriving in London in April 1764.

With the possible exceptions of Peking and Tokyo, London was then the largest city on earth, with a population of nearly a million. Within Mozart's lifetime, Great Britain changed from an agricultural nation of seven million to a commercial and industrial one almost twice as populous; a major transformation of unprecedented speed. The process was well underway when Wolfgang arrived in the capital; later that year, James Watt invented the steam engine.

The children played for King George III and Queen Charlotte. Both were music lovers, and Wolfgang even accompanied the queen as she sang. George III suffered from porphyria, an inherited metabolic disorder; he spent his last twenty years violently insane.

When they were not busy delighting British nobility, the children were taken to public concerts, already an established feature of London's musical life. Wolfgang heard some of Handel's oratorios—possibly *Messiah*—by today's standards the greatest music he had yet heard. The continued performances of Handel's choral masterpieces in Britain is an exception to the general neglect of baroque music at the time.

And Wolfgang made a friend who became his musical mentor: John Christian Bach, eleventh and youngest son of Johann Sebastian. Then twenty-eight, Christian Bach was an outstanding exponent of the galant style. He and Wolfgang took to each other immediately, spending hours improvising together at the keyboard. Much of Mozart's earliest music sounds just like the English Bach's: the same kinds of tunes, light and graceful, somewhat superficial. Several keyboard works ascribed to Mozart were later discovered to be Christian Bach's. The elegant quality stayed in Mozart's music, increasingly enriched by other, more interesting ones.

When the aristocracy left London for the summer, Leopold turned to the middle class, already sizable and prosperous. These people paid to hear concerts and even subscribed in advance; Handel wrote *Messiah* for this audience. Leopold himself wrote the ads that appeared in the London newspapers, which unhesitatingly described Wolfgang as "the greatest prodigy that Europe or even human nature has to boast of" and guaranteed that "everybody will be astonished to hear a child of such tender age playing the harpsichord in such perfection. It surpasses all understanding and all imagination." Tickets cost as little as two and a half shillings, and Leopold, who billed himself as "the father of this miracle," made a bundle. The concerts extended into 1765.

In May of that year, in Virginia, Patrick Henry denounced King George III: "If this be treason, make the most of it."

Just before leaving London in June, Wolfgang was studied by Daines Barrington, a scholar and scientist. He wanted to know how the boy worked, what made the wonderful machine go. He collected all the facts available, even sending to Salzburg for verification of Wolfgang's birthdate. His published report was based on first-hand observations of Wolfgang alone and with his father.

Wolfgang was learning the difference between work and play. At first all his musical activities had been fun. Gradually he realized that he was supposed to be pleasing other people. Barrington noticed "a certain defiance" when Wolfgang had to prove his abilities instead of amusing himself. At eight he was a public figure, living up to other people's expectations.

Barrington found more than musical skill in the boy—he saw his complete absorption in music. When he played an aria, he sang passionately in his "thin and infantile" voice. At Barrington's request, he improvised love music and anger music, getting so carried away with rage that he "beat his harpsichord like a person possessed." While playing duets with his father, Wolfgang "looked back with some anger" when Leopold flubbed a passage, and then corrected him.

He also was a child who suddenly stopped playing and "ran about the room with a stick between his legs by way of a horse."

According to Barrington, Wolfgang was frequently "visited with musical ideas" in the middle of the night, which would wake him up. He would then go to the harpsichord and play. Most people have had a tune stuck in their heads at some time; Wolfgang, a composer, heard as yet unwritten music.

Everyone who met the child Wolfgang commented on his seriousness (and everyone who met the adult Mozart commented on his childlikeness). That seriousness probably saved him from becoming a destroyed human being, ruined by the publicity, pampering, and glitter of his childhood among strangers. Where his dignity came from is as hard to imagine as where he got his talent.

Leopold became seriously ill in the summer of 1764; that and Wolfgang's success extended the London tour to more than a year. While Leopold was sick, his son composed, dedicating sonatas to the queen; he was to compose continuously from then on.

In all, Mozart wrote between six hundred and seven hundred works, and only about seventy were published in his lifetime. Different publishers numbered his compositions as they liked, resulting in duplications of opus numbers. And Mozart didn't date his compositions, or even list them, until 1784.

The first complete chronological catalogue of Mozart's works was assembled in 1862 by Ludwig von Köchel, who had previously catalogued plants and minerals. He dated each piece, using its style and Mozart's musical handwriting as guides. Each was assigned a number based on its date of composition, preceded by the letter *K* (for Köchel). K. 1 is a minuet Wolfgang wrote at home in 1762; the sonatas for

Versailles.

the queen of England are K. 6-9. Each work has its own number, whether it is a three-minute song or a four-hour opera. The last number, K. 626, is the requiem Mozart was composing when he died.

Köchel's original catalogue has been revised several times. New Mozart works have been found, more accurate dates derived, and works thought to be by Mozart correctly identified as someone else's. The original Köchel numbers had become too familiar to change, so new works were squeezed in (K. 285a) and a not quite exact chronology remains. Every time a work of Mozart's is performed or broadcast, its Köchel number is given along with its title.

In the fall of 1765, Leopold took his family to Holland. A successful series of concerts was cut short when Nannerl came down with typhoid fever; she was so sick that last rites were administered. Wolfgang performed alone, for the first time presenting a concert entirely of original works. No sooner did Nannerl recover than Wolfgang caught the same disease. For two months he lingered, sometimes delirious, sometimes in a coma. But he recovered and was playing again on his tenth birthday.

The grand tour concluded in triumph: a return engagement at Versailles (where one spectator wrote, "if these children live, monarchs will vie for their possession"), concerts throughout Switzerland and southern Germany, then home to Salzburg at the end of November 1766. The family's fame had arrived first, the local newspapers faithfully recording the conquests of Vienna, Paris, and London. It was just the kind of story to accompany the news of the latest technological advances; as one music lover wrote, "Dear God, it is incredible how far all the sciences have advanced!"

For Leopold Mozart, the tour had vindicated all his beliefs. But the large sums of money he had taken in at the London concerts had been used up in travel expenses, and new appearances were necessary. "God daily works new miracles in this child," Leopold wrote, and he was determined to push the miracles along.

He began a period of intensive musical training for his son. Wolfgang practiced harpsichord and violin and studied formal counterpoint, the science of writing independent melody lines that are played simultaneously. Wolfgang's aptitude for foreign languages was already evident; his French and Italian were fluent, his English not bad. Leopold also taught mathematics in this university of one, and Wolfgang was enthusiastic. He covered the whole house with chalk figures when he worked out a problem. Like music, mathematics concerns order, rules, harmony, and inspiration. For fun, Wolfgang participated in the family's favorite pastime, air-gun shooting.

Wolfgang never forgot the grand tour (maybe he wished he could). He was applauded, marveled at, adored everywhere, the center of attention. And all for doing what he loved best: playing and composing music. Whatever glory he achieved as an adult—and he knew many glorious moments—were in the shadow of his spectacular childhood. It is not surprising that a kind of yearning, perhaps a nostalgia, entered Mozart's music early on and remained until the end.

He began composing again as soon as he was home, especially since the archbishop was eager to test his reputation. Just eleven, he wrote a few keyboard concertos adopted from other composers' works, and his first stage piece, a Latin comedy for the university. Wolfgang loved setting words to music best of all, perhaps because of the power of his apparently innate sense of drama and his emotional exuberance.

In September, Leopold took his family back to Vienna, fully expecting another round of successes. Instead the trip was a flop, the first for Wolfgang but not the last.

The court was celebrating the upcoming marriage of one of the empress's daughters, and Leopold thought Wolfgang would perform, or even compose, for the occasion. But a smallpox epidemic broke out in the city, and the sixteen-year-old bride-to-be died. The Mozarts left town. Leopold could have had his children inoculated, a procedure then in its infancy (thirty years later Lister perfected it), but it contradicted his religious beliefs. God gave and God took away, especially in the case of miracle children.

Both children got smallpox. Wolfgang suffered particularly; his eyes covered with pustules, he was virtually blind for a week. (Both Bach and Handel went blind at the end of their lives, at least partly from endless hours writing music by candlelight.) But Wolfgang's sight was restored, and he spent relaxed hours learning card tricks and fencing, two lifelong hobbies, while recuperating.

The Mozarts returned to Vienna in January 1768. The beautiful boy wonder was no longer beautiful (his pockmarks were permanent), no longer new, and at twelve practically no longer a boy. The court was still in mourning, and the aristocrats were no longer interested: they had already seen him, the sensation was over, his scars looked ugly. And from Salzburg came word that the archbishop had cut off Leopold's salary.

Then Emperor Joseph II, Maria Theresa's son and co-ruler, commissioned Wolfgang to write a comic opera, in Italian, for the court opera. Italian comic

Wolfgang, age 12.

opera was extremely popular in Vienna, and most of the operatic composers and musicians were Italian (Austria controlled most of Italy at the time). Italian comic opera featured stock characters in stock situations—clever servants outwitting stupid masters, lecherous old men attempting to marry beautiful young women, disguises, mistaken identities, happy endings. The emphasis was on wit, visual humor, and above all, singable tunes.

Wolfgang wrote his first opera in three months, setting a tale of amorous adventure that could not have had much meaning to him then. Its production was delayed, and in the end it was not performed at all. Leopold claimed jealous musicians had conspired against his son. Rumors abounded: the music was no good, the music was very good but Leopold had written it, famous singers refused to sing a child's music, the whole thing was a fraud. Leopold was furious and bitter; what could Wolfgang have thought? He knew his music was good; what had gone wrong?

He wrote another one: this time a German-language operetta, a musical comedy with spoken dialogue and songs, based on a story by Rousseau. Commissioned by Franz Mesmer, who treated mental illness with magnets and hypnosis, *Bastien and Bastienne* (K. 50) is still performed. A musical coincidence: a theme in its introduction anticipates the theme Beethoven used to begin his Third Symphony, the *Eroica,* composed in 1803.

Wolfgang's first large-scale work was a mass he composed for the opening of an orphanage in Vienna. He conducted his *Orphanage* Mass (K. 139, more accurately K. 47a) to a full house, including the empress, in December 1768, a month before he turned thirteen. For a long time the music to this mass was presumed lost, and what is now thought to be the *Orphanage* Mass was assigned to 1772 (hence its higher Köchel number). It was considered impossible that any twelve-year-old, even Mozart, could have written so impressive and moving a work.

The mass lasts forty-five minutes and uses four soloists, chorus, strings, oboes, trumpets and trombones (sometimes muted), and drum. Like most contemporary masses, its style is operatic, the text set dramatically; the section "He was crucified" is somber and mournful, "He rose again" joyous and blazing. In places the chorus sings great serious fugues, then a soprano sings what could be a love song. The orchestration is brilliant.

In 1903, the Roman Catholic Church banned church performances of all instrumental masses, including Mozart's, Haydn's, Beethoven's, Schubert's, and Bruckner's, on the grounds that the music called attention to itself and away from divine worship. Gregorian chant was restored, discreetly accompanied by organ. The churches built in Mozart's day—multicolored, fancifully ornamented, cheerful places—still stand; the church music is sometimes heard in concert, but survives (if at all), like so much music of the past, on records.

Leopold Mozart realized the astonishing musical growth in his son's work, and he determined to take the boy to the homeland of opera, Italy. The only road to real success open to eighteenth-century musicians was opera; orchestral programs in enormous concert halls was a nineteenth-century phenomenon.

Opera had begun in Italy in the early 1600s as an attempt to re-create classic Greek drama, which was known to have had musical accompaniment. The earliest operas took subjects from Greek mythology; the most popular was Orpheus, the personification of music who brought his dead wife back from hell by the power of his song. In the eighteenth century, historical subjects were popular—though not those from current history: Julius Caesar was safer. So-called serious operas invariably attached a happy ending to all the noble goings-on. The music was divided into recitative, declamatory and speech-inflected, and aria, elaborate song. Ballets and marches were liberally interspersed. Operas were written in either Italian or French, although there were early attempts, including Purcell's *Dido and Aeneas* in 1690, at English opera. Like Mozart, Purcell died at thirty-five.

Italians had also pioneered in orchestral writing; early symphonies and concertos were patterned on opera overtures. Vivaldi and Corelli had created an instrumental style much admired (and copied) by Bach and Handel. A trip to Italy was a musical necessity.

Leopold and Wolfgang left for Italy in December 1769; Nannerl stayed home with her mother. There was only room for one Mozart now, Leopold reasoned, and he felt Nannerl would detract from Wolfgang. She was eighteen and an excellent musician who had shared in the glory of the grand tour. If she felt hurt at being left behind she never mentioned it—in so many words. She was not the first or the last daughter to be passed over for a son.

Because of the family separation, Wolfgang wrote letters to his sister and mother. Leopold insisted that all letters, including his own, be saved. He had no doubt but that Mozart's name belonged to the history of music. Leopold Mozart planned to write a biography of his son; significantly, he never did.

The letters of Wolfgang and his family—more than six hundred of them—were first published in English in 1938. They make wonderful reading, ideal with Mozart's music as accompaniment. Almost all Wolfgang's letters were to his family; none was to another musician or celebrity. They were full of gossip, character studies of the many people he met and observed. Wolfgang delighted in puns, anagrams, and all kinds of jokes; he wrote in several languages in the same letter, and often illustrated his tales with music or drawings. His handwriting was sloppy ("I write like pigs piss") and the letters were ink-stained and messy. Like his music, his letters were not written for posterity, yet even they endure.

Wolfgang was delighted with the Italian trip from the start. He was no longer a child prodigy, but a young musician with impressive credentials, to be taken seriously—but not too seriously. "I have no news except that Herr Gellert, the poet, has died," the fourteen-year-old wrote his sister, "and has written no more poetry since his death."

The splendors of the Italian countryside meant little to Wolfgang; cities interested him, with their crowds and music. Little if any of Mozart's music suggests the mountains or the sea. The only nature that appealed to him was human nature.

From their first stop, Verona, Wolfgang and Leopold were met by Italy's leading musicians and teachers, instead of the usual array of petty nobility. Music was everywhere, and the travelers heard Italian opera almost every night, with its long flowing melodies and sensuous sound. In Milan, Wolfgang was commissioned to write a serious opera for the coming season.

On March 5, 1770, British soldiers fired into a crowd of angry Bostonians, killing several; Samuel Adams called it the Boston Massacre.

While performing in Florence that spring, Wolfgang met a friend: the first real friend he ever had. Thomas Linley, exactly Wolfgang's age, had come to Florence from London to study violin. They played duets and compared their experiences, musical and otherwise. Wolfgang wept when it came time to leave; Linley had a sonnet written to express his affection. Wolfgang never forgot this special friend, who drowned in a boating accident when he was twenty-two.

Father and son traveled on, over the bad roads, staying in the "most horrible, filthy inns, where we get nothing to eat except here and there eggs and broccoli,"

Wolfgang wearing his papal decoration.

as Leopold grumbled. The two of them arrived in Rome on Ash Wednesday, 1770.

In Rome, Wolfgang made himself known through a musical feat that combined great learning with show-business flair. The Sistine Chapel had as its exclusive property a setting of the Miserere (Psalm 51), which was not allowed to be copied under threat of excommunication. It was a complex vocal work in four and five parts, concluding with a nine-part chorus. After one hearing, Wolfgang wrote out the score from memory with astonishing accuracy. The only consequence was added publicity.

Of his visit to Saint Peter's, Wolfgang wrote Nannerl, "I have had the honor of kissing St. Peter's foot and as I have the misfortune to be so small someone had to lift up the undersigned old rascal." Filled with Italy, he signed his letters Wolfgango Amadeo di Mozartini.

After Rome came Naples, then Italy's most populous city and the center of Italian opera. When Wolfgang performed, rumor spread among the more superstitious that his powers came from black magic in the form of a ring. Naturally Wolfgang removed the ring with a flourish and conquered the skeptics. More blasé than impressed, he wrote home "Vesuvius is smoking furiously today, thunder and lightning and all the rest."

When they returned to Rome, Wolfgang was awarded the highest decoration he was ever to receive: the pope made him a knight of the Order of the Golden Spur, an honor only two musicians had previously attained. The pope granted an audience to the new cavalier, "whom we understand to have excelled since thy earliest youth in the sweetest sounding of the harpsichord."

In this period of European feudalism when titles meant so much, Wolfgang never used his title and seldom wore the decoration. Perhaps some of the egalitarian ideas floating around the intellectual circles in which he moved had reached him; maybe he had seen enough of the nobility to be uninterested in joining in their pretenses. Probably he was too proud to use anything but his name. The decoration itself, a gold cross with matching spurs, wound up in a pawn shop.

Back to Bologna, where Wolfgang studied counterpoint with Padre Martini, considered Europe's finest music theorist and teacher. After three months Wolfgang was elected a member of the philharmonic society, the youngest ever to be so honored. Recognition from other musicians meant more to him than papal medals, and he kept his diploma till the end of his life.

That summer, James Cook became the first European to visit Australia, which he claimed for George III of Great Britain.

While Wolfgang worked on his opera in Milan, Leopold noticed that the boy was growing, and that his broken voice prevented him from singing as he composed, which he liked to do. (Fifteen years later, Mozart captured the onrush of teenage sexuality to perfection in the character of Cherubino in *The Marriage of Figaro*.) Love—with music Mozart's whole life—was from now on sexual.

The Milanese opera was a complete success: twenty performances, standing room only, turned-away crowds, encores and bravos. Applause ringing in his ears and a new commission in his pocket, the happy composer and his proud father returned to Salzburg in March 1771. Perhaps in his honor his mother cooked his favorite dish, liver dumplings and sauerkraut.

In August, Wolfgang and Leopold were back in Milan, Wolfgang preparing a new opera to celebrate the wedding of Archduke Ferdinand, another child of Maria Theresa. Conditions were ideal, Wolfgang wrote to Nannerl. "Upstairs we have a violinist, downstairs another one, in the next room a singing master who gives lessons, in the other room opposite ours an oboist. That's great fun when you're composing! It gives you plenty of ideas."

He wasn't just joking. Throughout his life Mozart was exceptional both in his ability to assimilate any style of writing and in selecting what would influence him. From beginning to end, however, he maintained an individual voice. Some of his melodies can be traced, in varying degrees of refinement, over twenty years of creative work.

The new opera was a success, and Archduke Ferdinand, probably at Leopold Mozart's urging, considered appointing the father and son as court musicians in Milan. First he wrote to Maria Theresa, the recipient of Wolfgang's wet kisses nine years before. She advised her son against "burdening yourself with useless people . . . . It degrades your service when these people go about the world like beggars." Herself the mother of sixteen children, the empress added, "Besides, he has a large family." Wolfgang didn't get the job.

Leopold Mozart was angry. He was usually unhappy and grumbling, discontent wherever he went. His two obsessive complaints were how little money he had and how badly his son was treated. "He idolizes his son a little too much, and thus does all he can to spoil him," one composer wrote, adding that "the boy's natural good sense" would save Wolfgang from his father's excesses.

Back in Salzburg by December 1771, Wolfgang composed steadily. A new prince-archbishop, Count Colloredo, had been elected, and the young composer wrote pageant music for his coronation. Wolfgang also composed instrumental music for the prince-archbishop's orchestra and held the title court composer.

The music Mozart wrote as a teenager in Salzburg is seldom heard in concerts, but most of it is available on records. Mozart is the most frequently recorded classical composer, and someday, no doubt, record collectors will be able to have every note of his surviving music. Then Mozart's music can be heard in the order he wrote it, instead of the usual, backwards way of hearing late, great works first. Because his early music contains so many anticipations of his mature works, it is difficult to distinguish the pieces as they are from what they become. But there is no difficulty in hearing how beautiful many of them are.

For instance, by 1772 Wolfgang had written more than twenty symphonies; in all he completed about fifty, of which forty remain. (Haydn wrote 104 symphonies, but he lived twice as long.) Mozart's symphonies are not huge heaven-stormers like Beethoven's or Mahler's; only his last symphonies are intense and personal. His early symphonies are twenty-minute long, three-movement pieces modeled on Italian opera overtures. The three movements are fast, slow, fast (French overtures are the opposite), festive and ceremonial in style, good for opening or closing an evening of music, not for the main course. What Mozart's early symphonies do have are arresting tunes, liveliness and spirit, and the unexpected: a quick change in harmony, a trick with rhythm, a warm, sweet sound. Two in particular are rich in melodic ideas, especially in their first movements: Symphony no. 14 (K. 114) and Symphony no. 20 (K. 133).

Perhaps these works would never be heard if Mozart had died in 1772. Until the 1950s brought a Mozart revival on records, most of his early works were known only to musicians, who could read scores.

The other kind of instrumental music Wolfgang wrote was music for festive occasions, light and dancy, to be played outdoors while people ate, talked, or idled about. These suites, known as serenades, divertimentos, cassations, or night music, were longer than symphonies, often containing two slow movements and various dance movements between the fast opening and finale. Generally the whole piece was not heard at once, but a movement at a time. The Divertimento for Strings (K. 136) embodies the young Mozart's clarity, brilliance, and sensuality.

The summer he wrote it he was in love with the daughter of a court official, who stirred up his sixteen-year-old's blood. This was also the summer that Austria, Prussia, and Russia began to gobble up Poland, until by 1796 it was all gone.

The music Wolfgang was writing combined the melodic beauties of Italian opera with the formal structures of the German masters Leopold had taught him. He wrote in the same style his contemporaries did, but, with the exception of Haydn's, his music sounds better. It is partly a matter of melody: Mozart's tunes are not just pretty, they are suggestive. They are full of emotional reminders, of meaning underneath the shimmer. The melodies insinuate their way to the heart. Within a traditional pattern, new musical life emerges.

In November 1772, Wolfgang and Leopold returned to Italy for the third and last time. Shortly before they left, a court in Aix-en-Provence sentenced the Marquis de Sade to death in absentia for "crimes of poisoning and sodomy."

Wolfgang's third annual Italian opera was well received, and for the star, a castrato, he wrote *Exsultate, jubilate* (K. 165), a setting of a sacred Latin text as a twenty-minute concerto for voice and orchestra. Still frequently performed (although sung by soprano, whose range, but not timbre, is the same as a castrato's), it concludes with a fast finale in which only word, "Allelulia," is sung. Singing one word for ten minutes could be most boring, but Mozart's melody, climaxing on a high C, is exhilarating. Whenever there's something to celebrate, this is the perfect music. It is the earliest Mozart work that sounds fully Mozartean.

When Wolfgang and Leopold returned to Salzburg in March 1773, the future seemed assured. The Italian tours had given Wolfgang a new self-confidence and an independent artistic identity. At seventeen he had composed six operas, of which three had been performed with acclaim in Italy, opera's homeland; twenty symphonies; eight string quartets; numerous masses, smaller church pieces, and serenades. Though not an astonishingly large output by eighteenth-century standards (Telemann, who died when Mozart was eleven, had more than a thousand compositions to his name), it certainly is an impressive one. No composer living then, except perhaps Haydn, could have composed the best of them. Wolfgang was unparalleled as a virtuoso instrumentalist; crowned heads had received him in palaces from London to Naples. He had gained recognition in a highly competitive profession. All he lacked was a good position at some important court.

The next four years were not what he expected. After a vain attempt to be appointed in Vienna ("Her Majesty the empress was very gracious to us, but that was all," wrote Leopold), Wolfgang remained in the service of the prince-archbishop of Salzburg. He came to hate both man and town more with every passing day.

Compared to Vienna, Paris, and London, Salzburg was a backwater town. Its petty nobility were just that: schemers and time wasters. Wolfgang was bored.

As for Prince-Archbishop Colloredo, Wolfgang soon despised "the old prick." Colloredo considered himself an enlightened liberal; he kept a bust of Voltaire, widely considered an atheist, on his desk. He loved music and was an amateur violinist. But his basic human attitudes were feudal: he was a prince, Wolfgang was his servant, a servant was a thing.

Colloredo expected Wolfgang to provide him and his court with suitably entertaining music. What the composer wanted to write was of absolutely no concern. Wolfgang felt his employer was envious of his talent and reputation, and didn't want his servant to forget his place. Mozart later set to music the following words of an angry count: "Shall I live to see a servant of mine happy and enjoying pleasure that I desire in vain?"

The times were right for the young composer, newly intoxicated with adulthood. Throughout Europe the ideas of romanticism were spreading, with their emphasis on heightened personal expressiveness. In 1774, Goethe's first novel, *The Sorrows of Young Werther,* became the first European best seller. It tells the story of a passionate, sensitive young man, misunderstood and alienated, who loses the woman he loves and then kills himself. *Werther* was so influential that an epidemic of suicides among sensitive young men of the upper classes resulted. The novel captured a feeling of deep discontent and unfulfilled yearnings in a society committed to the superficial. Wolfgang may never have read *Werther,* though he must certainly have heard about it in the fashionable homes he frequented. And he was a sensitive young man in an environment accurately described by Goethe.

The music Wolfgang wrote in 1774 reflects a more brooding, restless quality. When in Vienna, he had heard some of Haydn's symphonies, and he integrated their power into his own sound, still basically elegant and operatic. One result is his Symphony no. 25 (K. 183), sometimes called his first "great" or even "late" symphony (he was seventeen when he wrote it). It is his first symphony in a minor key, which gives it a sad, and in this case anguished sound; not the kind of music to open a concert of light tunes. The sense of urgency and foreboding is emphasized by extreme contrasts of loud and soft. The music's inner tension is striking, and remains a feature of Mozart's music.

Two other works of this year are still popular. At the request of a local soloist, Wolfgang wrote three bassoon concertos, only one of which survived (K. 191); the low-lying, odd-sounding bassoon is seldom used as a solo instrument. The concerto's slow middle movement starts with a theme that Wolfgang liked: he first wrote it down in his London notebook when he was eight, and later used it for an aria in *The Marriage of Figaro*. Most of Mozart's slow movements suggest singing, and he used the same themes freely across different forms. His Symphony no. 29 (K. 201) sums up his achievements in orchestral writing at the time. Its opening theme is one of the catchiest he ever wrote, and its finale is like a hundred fountains shooting off at once.

Wolfgang most of all wanted to write another opera, which was impossible in tiny Salzburg. Fortunately the elector of Bavaria commissioned a comic opera from him for the annual Munich winter carnival in 1775. Leopold and Nannerl were in the full house when *The Pretended Gardener* (K. 196) was performed in January. The story is ridiculous, but much of the music is haunting. In one scene, a character speaks in different languages, and the music mirrors the words with different national styles. Wolfgang wrote to his mother that "it is impossible for me to describe the applause," but there was no job offer or new commission. His mastery was recognized; a leading poet wrote, "If Mozart has not been forced like some hothouse plant, he must surely become one of the world's greatest composers."

In April 1775, the American Revolution began at Lexington and Concord. Rousseau's words were being set to a different music.

Wolfgang was working on a new project—violin concertos. He composed five by the end of the year, and he never wrote any others. He wrote them for himself as soloist. Leopold urged his son to practice the violin, Leopold's instrument, because he wanted him to become "the first violinist of Europe," a typically grandiose desire. But Wolfgang preferred the keyboard, especially the new piano, as his solo instrument, and among strings he favored the mellow-sounding viola.

The violin concertos set the standard for all Mozart's subsequent concertos. They follow the fast-slow-fast pattern and feature exciting openings, singing slow movements (the violin at its most vocal), and dazzling, joyful finales. There is such a profusion of melodies that some listeners found the concertos hard to appreciate because too much was happening. Particularly beautiful are the first (K. 207), fourth (K. 218), and fifth (K. 219) concertos. The fifth ends with music in what was called Turkish style; Wolfgang adapted it from a harem ballet in one of his Milanese operas. It sounds more Hungarian than Turkish: gypsy music, fiery and mock angry, the European epitome of exoticism.

Within these concertos Mozart's personal voice is unmistakable. He is one of the most distinctive and easily identifiable of all composers. As he matured his music became more refined, clearer, richer, and more intense, but it always sounds like Mozart. That music written in such traditional forms sounds so personal, fresh, and moving is one of the central contradictions of Mozart's artistic life.

As Salzburg concertmaster, Wolfgang composed, conducted, and performed for a low yearly salary. He wrote for specific occasions: royal visits, funerals, weddings, birthdays. Hundreds of other concertmasters in small courts across the continent wrote such music endlessly, mass-produced throwaway music. Yet under the same circumstances Bach and Haydn created music of lasting beauty. So did Mozart, however much he hated his dependence.

In 1776, the year of the Declaration of Independence, Wolfgang composed some of his loveliest music. The Serenade no. 6 (K. 239, "Serenata notturna") divides the orchestra in two, each section placed in opposite corners of a large room for an early stereo effect. For the wedding of the mayor's daughter, Wolfgang composed an enormous serenade, known by the mayor's name, Haffner. All Salzburg's elite were at the wedding, and Wolfgang wanted to dazzle them with his brilliance, and he did. The *Haffner* Serenade (K. 250) lasts close to an hour, its eight movements comprising a small violin concerto as well as the usual dances. All that was needed were pretty tunes; Wolfgang delighted in showing off in what is one of the greatest of all his works. It sounds especially wonderful early on New Year's Eve. Three outstanding examples of Mozart's lighter style are the Divertimentos no. 10 (K. 247), no. 11 (K. 251), and no. 15 (K. 287), the second written as a twenty-fifth birthday present for Nannerl, who was earning a living giving music lessons. Its

French style was perhaps to remind her of their happy days as child prodigies in Paris twelve years before.

In comparison to what Mozart wrote later, these works are indeed light and "early," but they are not inferior. Any of them may contain a special phrase or tune that becomes someone's favorite.

Wolfgang also produced his first great keyboard concerto, no. 9 (K. 271), for a visiting French virtuoso, Mlle. Jeunehomme, after whom it is sometimes called. His earlier concertos, probably conceived for the harpsichord, are tuneful enough; this one is heroic. The solo instrument (nowadays generally a piano) enters in the second bar, without waiting for the usual orchestral introduction. The concerto is full of contrasts: between the dramatic outer movements and the yearning middle movement, between soloist and orchestra. Written almost exactly on his twenty-first birthday, this concerto is the prototype of the great works in the form from Beethoven's to Rachmaninoff's.

Wolfgang was getting nowhere in Salzburg; the prince-archbishop bluntly told him he had no future there. Colloredo found Wolfgang arrogant and uncooperative, and Wolfgang felt tyrannized and underappreciated. In August 1777, he petitioned his employer for permission to travel "to enable us to make some money" while finding a more suitable position. Colloredo refused. Wolfgang and Leopold asked again; this time Colloredo fired them both. Leopold quickly got himself reinstated, but Wolfgang decided to stay fired and take to the road again, throughout Germany and finally to Paris.

Leopold Mozart had to stay in Salzburg. For twenty-one years father and son had spent every day together, and now they were to be separated for the first time. It was small consolation to him that his wife would accompany their son. Only Leopold knew what was best for Wolfgang, only Leopold could steer his career and save him from flatterers, chiselers, and women, the triple threat that awaited the impressionable, romantic Wolfgang everywhere. But there was no choice.

In September, Wolfgang and his mother left Salzburg. As Leopold wrote, "I made great efforts to control myself in order not to make our parting too painful." Later he "sat for a long time without thinking of anything" on "that sad day I never thought I should have to face."

Leopold had good reason to be miserable. Wolfgang came back a changed man, bolder and freer than Leopold could have imagined. And Maria Anna Mozart didn't come back at all.

3.

Down and Out

Perhaps he thinks people remain twelve years old forever.
—Mozart, 1778

The first stop on the new tour was Munich, where *The Pretended Gardener* had been so successful just two years earlier. He finally got an interview with the elector of Bavaria, and in flowery language told how it was his fondest dream to serve this illustrious prince who was such a . . . . "Yes, my dear boy, but I have no vacancy," the ruler interrupted. "If only there were a vacancy."

Wolfgang remained in Munich anyway, enjoying his first taste of independence from both father and boss. "I am quite a second Papa, for I see to everything," he wrote to Leopold, *"mon très cher père."* He gave concerts of his own works and for the first time in years felt appreciated. One music lover "kept on shouting 'bravo' where other noblemen would take a pinch of snuff, blow their noses, clear their throats, or start a conversation." Some of them had asked Wolfgang to stay in Munich without an appointment and be subsidized by subscriptions, a radical idea which would become standard within thirty years. Wolfgang was tempted, but Leopold vetoed the plan by mail: "how the archbishop would sneer." Wolfgang, who signed his letters to Leopold "your most obedient son," turned down the offer.

Leopold Mozart wrote to his son practically every day. The letters cover the entire range of Wolfgang's activities: what to think, even how to write letters. No detail was too small. In the same letter that Leopold described his heartbreak at seeing his son ride off, he reminds Wolfgang to have boot trees put in his boots overnight. If Mozart remained childlike throughout his life, it was Leopold's infantilizing that made it possible.

Wolfgang went on to Augsburg, his father's hometown. At one of his concerts a well-meaning admirer told him he was the image of his father.

Mother and son stayed with Leopold's brother and his family. They had a daughter Wolfgang's age, and the cousins immediately became good friends. "We both laugh at everyone and have great fun," he wrote Leopold. She had a reputation for being fast: Wolfgang wrote of a night when one of her admirers, a priest, had gotten drunk and begun singing her a love song. He had asked Wolfgang to join in, and the composer sang under his breath, "oh you idiot, lick my ass," much to his cousin's delight. Leopold glumly wrote back that "it seems to me she has too many friends among the priests." In the months that followed, Wolfgang frequently wrote to his cousin; all his letters to her are vulgar, suggestive, smutty, and good-natured: not the letters of an angelic child.

His concerts produced no results. He was already sick of the local gentry, "the Duchess Smackbottom, the Countess Makewater, to say nothing of the Princess Dunghill with her two daughters, who, however, are already married to the two Princes Potbelly von Pigtail." On his father's instructions, Wolfgang wore his papal medal, and some town bigshots teased him about it, asking him how much it had cost him and whether it was brass or tin. He seldom wore it again.

His greatest joy in Augsburg was meeting Andreas Stein, famous as a piano maker. Wolfgang fell in love with his instrument, the fortepiano, a predecessor to

Wolfgang's piano. The portraits on the wall are of Nannerl, the Mozart family, and Wolfgang.

A letter from Wolfgang to his cousin.

the grand piano. Its strings were not strung as tensely as those in a modern piano, and lighter, leather-wrapped hammers were used. Consequently its tone was light, with echoes of the harpsichord's pingy sound. Less muscle was needed to depress the keys, making clear articulation of fast passages possible. Mozart, probably the greatest pianist of his time, was never able to afford a Stein piano.

Stein had a daughter who was the latest child prodigy; she had made her debut the previous year at age seven. The ex-prodigy watched her play, no doubt with a rush of memories and mixed feelings. "Anyone who sees and hears her play and can keep from laughing must be made of stone, like her father," he wrote Leopold, punning on the name Stein, which means "stone." "She rolls her eyes and smirks," Wolfgang continued uncharitably, and in difficult sections "doesn't bother her head about it, but when the moment arrives, she just leaves out the notes, raises her hand and starts up again quite comfortably." The girl continued her career nonetheless, and later became Beethoven's close friend.

From Salzburg came angry letters, often centering on money. Leopold wasn't getting any younger, he ceaselessly reminded his son, and he had gone into debt; poor Nannerl was working too; and there Wolfgang was wasting his time, enjoying himself. Where was his sense of responsibility? Had he been going to confession?

The last question was easy—he had been. Wolfgang took his religion seriously, though without Leopold's sectarianism. When he thought about God he thought of "His love, His compassion, and His tenderness toward His creation." A God of love for a composer of love.

In Paris, Antoine Lavoisier discovered oxygen and explained its role in combustion. Fire was no longer a mystery.

After two unhappy weeks in Augsburg, Wolfgang arrived in Mannheim, then famous for having both the finest orchestra in Europe and one of the few German-language opera companies. The orchestral players were all virtuosos, at that time the exception, not the rule. The "Mannheim sound" featured explosive crescendos and breathtaking decrescendos, a technique then new. The orchestra included clarinets, the newest member of the woodwind choir. Wolfgang loved the clarinet's rich, haunting timbre, which reminded him (and many others) of the human voice. His last completed work, finished three months before his death, was a clarinet concerto.

Because of its musical reputation, Mannheim was Wolfgang's best hope. But no offers came, despite a successful series of concerts. Instead, he had to listen to the usual sophisticated foolishness. One patron of the arts told him "bad music never gets on my nerves; beautiful music does, and then I get a headache." Nor was money forthcoming. "Let me tell you, I now have five watches. I am therefore seriously thinking of having an additional watch pocket on each trouser leg so that when I visit some great lord, I shall wear both watches so that it will not occur to him to present me with another one." A baron graciously asked what he could do for the young genius, and when Wolfgang started to tell him, the baron quickly said "Money? Oh that I cannot do. But if there's anything else—?" Wolfgang's reply was to the point: "But there is *nothing else* you can do for me."

Some commissions did come in, and he took pupils. He wrote a piano sonata, no. 7 (K. 309), for one student, and he declared that its slow movement was her musical portrait—"she is exactly like the andante." A wealthy Dutchman asked Wolfgang for "three easy little concertos and a couple of quartets for flute," an instrument the composer detested. He composed late into the night after teaching, concertizing, and politicking all day. He finished one flute concerto (K. 313) and arranged an earlier oboe concerto for a second (K. 314), and he completed three flute quartets (flute, violin, viola, and cello, K. 285, K. App. 171, and K. 298). All use the flute brilliantly, despite Wolfgang's dislike. The Dutchman, something of a rip-off artist, paid Wolfgang half the agreed amount.

"I could, to be sure, scribble off things the whole day long," he complained to Leopold, "but a composition goes out into the world, and naturally I do not want to have cause to be ashamed of my name on the title page." Unsympathetic, Leopold advised him to write crowd pleasers and stop being so fussy.

The flute concerto marks the halfway point in Mozart's total musical output. He was just twenty-two.

Wolfgang stayed on in Mannheim. Leopold's letters grew fiercer; he reminded his son of how well the grand tour had gone under his management, and he protested that "your long and quite unnecessary sojourn has ruined all your prospects." As always, he stressed Wolfgang's destiny, "to win glory, honor, and money . . . to save his father from scornful mockery"—the mockery of the hated prince-archbishop, the common enemy. Wolfgang and Leopold used a cipher code whenever their letters mentioned "the archclown," since he could and did intercept and read the mail of any of his servants, including the Mozarts.

That winter, 1777–1778, Washington's troops froze at Valley Forge.

By February Leopold's patience ran out. His son's letters were filled with jokes and endearments, but no explanation of his long stay. Finally the reason became clear—Wolfgang had fallen passionately in love. Her name was Aloysia Weber, the second of four daughters of a Mannheim music copyist. She was sixteen, pretty, and sang "spendidly, with a pure, lovely voice," the lover wrote to his father. He composed songs and arias for her, which she sang with deep feeling. All she needed was practice in acting and she would be the operatic toast of all Europe. Just a little help from an adoring and talented friend. And of course a tour of Italy, with someone who knew the ropes. It was all settled; Maria Anna Mozart, who felt "too old to undertake such a long journey to Paris," would return home to Salzburg, and Wolfgang would accompany his beloved and her family to Italy. Together they would create a sensation.

Leopold Mozart was thunderstruck. Everything he had worked for single-handedly, relentlessly for eighteen years was about to go down the drain. Wolfgang as a singer's accompanist! He hit back hard and fast. "I read your letter with amazement and horror," he began. He graphically reminded Wolfgang of his family's many sacrifices, how their lives revolved around his, so that he could achieve "a position of eminence such as no musician has ever attained"—no more, no less. It would be a sacrilege if Wolfgang threw away his talents. Decide, ordered Leopold, "whether you die as an ordinary musician, utterly forgotten by the world; whether, captured by some woman, you die bedded on straw in an attic full of starving children." Leopold did not pull punches when his son, his life, was at stake. "Off to Paris with you! And at once! Take your place among important people."

The very obedient son obeyed. His farewell to Aloysia was tearful; he may have remembered it when he wrote the heartbreaking farewell music in *Così fan tutte*. Like the heroes in that opera, he promised to remain faithful.

Wolfgang made no mention of Aloysia's younger sister, Constanze, then a girl of fifteen, later his wife.

Neither son nor mother looked forward to the trip to Paris, thirty-four stage stations away in a cold winter. They arrived in March 1778.

The following six months in Paris were the unhappiest in Wolfgang's life. The old regime was in its dying days; corruption, decay, and intrigue were everywhere, including the music world, then involved in a large feud around the opera composer Gluck. No one much noticed Wolfgang, who had entranced everyone when he was ten. His former sweetheart, Marie Antoinette, now queen of France, refused even to see him; she was probably too busy dressing up (or down) as a milkmaid and cavorting in the palatial hut she had built at Versailles. What could one expect from the woman whose place in history was assured by her remarking, when told the starving Parisians had no bread, "Let them eat cake." Indirectly the court offered Wolfgang the minor and low-paying post of organist at Versailles, which he turned down.

He gave lessons and concerts. He hated the harp as much as he hated the flute, and his first commission, from a duke whose daughter he taught, was for a concerto for flute and harp (K. 299). As if to make up for his lack of interest, he created a work of remarkable sweetness, using the harp's heavenly associations to suggest an earthly paradise. Its slow movement is as hauntingly evocative as anything he had yet written. The duke put off payment and ultimately didn't pay Wolfgang at all.

Wolfgang tried to get an opera commission. For a while it looked as if he'd set a libretto about Alexander the Great, but the plan fell through; it would have been interesting to hear the death scene of a thirty-three-year-old hero. Instead Wolfgang wrote a ballet for the Paris opera, which to his disgust the choreographer presented mixed with other music—"worthless old French tunes," wrote Wolfgang—to form an unsatisfying hodgepodge; a common musical custom at the time. Another custom was that only the choreographer received billing. *Les petits riens* (K. App. 10) tells of two lovely shepherdesses who love the same shepherd. At the climax, the presumed shepherd exposes a breast, revealing to her stunned admirers and the delighted audience that she is a woman. Perfect entertainment for the empty-minded nobility so soon to be swept away. Wolfgang's music is better than the story deserves; the score was immediately lost, but turned up in the opera's archives a century later, in 1872.

His instrumental works had little better luck. For a public concert he wrote an elaborate and beautiful *Sinfonia concertante* for Four Woodwinds and Orchestra (K. App. 9); when he arrived to conduct it he was told the score had "disappeared"

Marie Antoinette, queen of France.

and not been copied. Wolfgang's dismay was shared by the musicians, who had rehearsed the work and liked it. This score was also discovered a hundred years later.

At the end of May 1778, Wolfgang, both high-spirited by nature and Catholic by religion, wrote to his father, "I often wonder whether life is worth living—I don't find much pleasure in anything."

His mood improved when his new symphony, no. 31 (K. 297), was received "with great applause" at a public concert in June. Now called the *Paris* Symphony, it was Mozart's first symphonic composition for a large orchestra. When a Mozart symphony is performed today, someone must decide whether to use the smallish orchestra Mozart generally wrote for or the larger, modern-day orchestra which Mozart no doubt would have liked.

The two leaders of French thought died in 1778: Voltaire in May, Rousseau in July.

While Wolfgang worked, worried, and wondered where the magic had gone, Maria Anna sat alone, in miserable lodgings, "as if I were in prison," she wrote Leopold. She had no friends, spoke no French, had nothing to do but needlepoint and wait. The weather was bad, money was scarce (and Paris has always been expensive), and Wolfgang was depressed: not only was his career floundering, but Aloysia Weber seldom answered his ardent letters. Maria Anna's health was poor.

On July 3, 1778, following extensive bloodletting, Maria Anna Mozart died at the age of fifty-seven, her son at her side. The next day she was buried in Paris, mourned by Wolfgang and one of his few friends, a trumpeter.

Her death was the first deep personal tragedy Wolfgang experienced. That night he fired off two letters, contradictory yet complementary. The first, to his father and sister, opened with the news that "my dear mother is very ill" and that "I have resigned myself wholly to God's will." Then urging Leopold and Nannerl to "banish these sad thoughts," Wolfgang went on with a long, chatty, cheerful letter, full of details about the performance of his *Paris* Symphony and his chances at the opera. The second, to a family friend in Salzburg, asked him to break the news to Leopold and Nannerl. "This has been the saddest day of my life," Wolfgang wrote. "When her illness became dangerous, I prayed to God for only two things—a happy death for her, and strength and courage for myself."

Wolfgang was granted the "fortitude and composure" he sought. Within days he was working again, rewriting a new, more carefree slow movement to his *Paris* Symphony and composing a new symphony, which is lost. He certainly was not callow or hard-hearted; he sincerely felt that "Almighty God willed it thus." Wolfgang wrote to his father that his mother's death had been "very easy and beautiful," making him feel "that in a moment she had become so happy; for how much happier is she now than we are! Indeed I wished at that moment to depart with her."

He also wanted to stay alive. There was more music to write, and love to experience. Before the month was out, Wolfgang was working out a plan to get Aloysia Weber to Paris.

Leopold Mozart's reaction to his wife's death also combined the tearful and the resigned. "My tears almost prevent me from writing," his letter stated, and closed with a reminder to Wolfgang, "Make sure that none of your possessions is lost."

Among the music Wolfgang composed just after his mother's death is a Sonata for Violin and Piano (K. 304). Stark and spare, tense and grim, it sounds more like Beethoven, who was then a boy of eight. (There's an old musical witticism that if Mozart had lived longer he would have been Beethoven.) Perhaps this sonata expressed Wolfgang's despair, although the relation between a piece of music and a specific event or memory is complex and subtle. Mozart's music is expressive and communicative, but exactly what a given piece says is ambiguous and open to any listener's interpretation.

Another severe and tragic work is his Piano Sonata no. 8 (K. 310), also in a minor key. Its sorrowful theme is underlined by hammer blows, cries of pain. Like most of Mozart's music for solo piano, this sonata was meant both for Mozart's use at concerts and for amateurs to play at home. The piano was at first a household instrument, and its emergence as a concert star was largely due to Mozart's compositions and performances. His Piano Sonata no. 11 (K. 331) of the same time is bright and cheerful, ending with a so-called Turkish rondo, like his earlier violin concerto. Sometimes the rondo is heard alone, most memorably in the film *Wuthering Heights,* in which a crazed-looking harpsichordist tears through the piece with manic intensity, to great effect.

Compared to the piano music of Chopin and Liszt, Mozart's piano music is not technically difficult, and it is often used to teach beginners. But it is not easy to play Mozart beautifully; the clear lines and simple textures make wrong or missed notes jump out, and no fudging is possible. As pianist Artur Schnabel remarked, "Too easy for children, too difficult for adults." Sophisticated simplicity: another of the many Mozart paradoxes.

From a sympathetic Parisian friend, Leopold Mozart got an opinion as to why his son was not succeeding. "He is too trusting, too inactive, too easy to catch, too little intent on the means that may lead to fortune. To make an impression here one has to be artful, enterprising, daring. To make his fortune I wish he had but half his talent and twice his shrewdness." Neither the writer nor Leopold seemed to realize that Wolfgang was making a real fortune—of uniquely beautiful works which speak directly to people far removed from the Paris of 1778—precisely because he had more talent than shrewdness.

Leopold decided it was time for his son to return to Salzburg. A quick succession of letters lured Wolfgang back. Every method of persuasion was used, including the suggestion that a new post was available in Salzburg; the lament that Nannerl was "already twenty-seven and not provided for"; the veiled accusation that Wolfgang should have had his mother bled sooner (it is not known what disease she had, but the bleeding certainly killed her); and the cry of a lonely, widowed old man for his one delight, his precious genius. Leopold was nothing if not thorough.

Wolfgang left Paris in September. Stopping along the route to give concerts, he arrived in Mannheim in November. He failed again to find work at the German opera, and he found that the court, including its musical apparatus, had moved to Munich. Aloysia Weber had been hired as a singer and was there too. Wolfgang followed.

Dressed in mourning, Wolfgang appeared at his beloved's home. She jilted him, publicly and frivolously. Her career was going well and she had bigger things in mind than marriage to a struggling itinerant musician. Years later Aloysia reminisced about her rejection. She knew nothing of his great genius; she saw only "a little man."

Wolfgang responded in a typically dual way. He sat down at the piano and played a popular song, the words to which were "I will gladly leave the girl who doesn't want me." His cousin from Augsburg had met him in Munich, presumably to be a bridesmaid ("perhaps you will have a great role to play here," Wolfgang had written), and the two chums laughed their heads off. At the same time, a friend wrote to Leopold that Wolfgang was bereft and depressed, and he feared that "your reception of him may not be as tender as he wishes. His whole pleasure and delight are centered in his father and sister; apart from them the world holds nothing more for him." In his personality as in his music, the joyous and sad exist side by side, and often simultaneously.

In January 1779, Wolfgang reentered what he rightly considered his "Salzburg slavery," taking on the position of court organist. His first works upon returning form a complementary pair, like the two masks of comedy and tragedy. Both are concertos with two solos instruments. The Concerto for Two Pianos (K. 365), written for him and Nannerl, is cheerfully captivating, while the *Sinfonia concertante* for Violin and Viola (K. 364) is dark blue, passionate and shot through with pain. He continued to write festive outdoor music, increasingly adding serious feeling to what was meant to be merely entertaining. In his Serenade no. 9 (K. 320) he adds a posthorn, a kind of hunting horn used by coach drivers to announce their arrival; Wolfgang had had plenty of opportunities to hear its sound, and he may have delighted in annoying Archbishop Colloredo with a sonic reminder of his urge to travel. He wrote a mass for the coronation of an allegedly miraculous picture of the Virgin Mary outside Salzburg, but the glorious music of the *Coronation* Mass (K. 317) sounds operatic, and the melody used in the Agnus Dei turns up as a haunting love aria in *The Marriage of Figaro*. And he finished off this period with two new symphonies. Symphony no. 33 (K. 319), one of the few symphonies to be published in his lifetime, is majestic and proud, and Symphony no. 34 (K. 338), written in 1780, ends with a madly energetic, whirling dance that sweeps away everything in its path, including gloomy spirits.

Wolfgang was satisfied with what he written, but restless and unfulfilled. He was eager to write another opera. "I am beside myself as soon as I hear anybody talk about an opera, sit in a theater, or hear singing," he had written to his father. "You know my greatest longing—to write operas."

In autumn 1780, a company of German actors played Salzburg. Led by Emanuel Schikaneder, who may have been the first German-speaking Hamlet, the troupe performed Shakespeare and contemporary plays, including Beaumarchais's *The Barber of Seville*. Wolfgang's mind turned more and more toward the theater; both Beaumarchais and Schikaneder later played key roles in Mozart's operatic output. As for *Hamlet,* Wolfgang felt "if the ghost's speech were not so long, it would make a better effect."

Financial gain and widespread popularity were not the main reasons for Wolfgang's opera mania. Opera combined the resources of a large orchestra (larger and more colorful than other instrumental ensembles), dance, and spectacle with the challenge of creating characters, giving them an emotional life through music, and, in doing so, there was the opportunity to move thousands of people at once. Insofar as any musical form commanded a "mass" audience in the eighteenth century, it was opera. Opera was a relatively new and vital genre then, despite its many conventions and stereotypes.

Munich came through: the elector of Bavaria commissioned a serious opera on the often-set story of Idomeneo, the mythical king of Crete during the Trojan War. Although Archbishop Colloredo resented his servant's traveling outside Salzburg to further his career, he could do nothing because he was outranked.

As was the common practice, Wolfgang was simply handed a finished libretto and proceeded to write music. He went to Munich to complete the opera in November.

Aloysia Weber wasn't there. She and her family had moved to Vienna, where late in October she married Joseph Lange, a court actor and painter. Lange later painted a portrait of Mozart which his wife said was the composer's closest likeness.

Wolfgang worked with great enthusiasm. Not that there weren't problems. The libretto was too long and undramatic, and the librettist refused to make cuts. Wolfgang solved the impasse by setting what he wanted but having the entire libretto printed. The title role was assigned to Anton Raaff, once the most famous tenor in Europe. In 1780, Raaff was sixty-six, and he had trouble breathing, let alone singing. Furthermore, he was full of unwanted condescending advice for the young composer, and he objected violently to singing in a quartet. Up to that time, opera traditionally used only solo arias and duets in which two voices sang the same melody in different registers. Wolfgang wrote a quartet in which four people sang different (though of course harmonically related) melodies at the same time, each one illustrating the character's state of mind. Wolfgang won out, and operatic quartets, quintets, and sextets rapidly became operatic staples.

The other leading male role was taken by a sixteen-year-old castrato ("*mio molto amato castrato,*" Wolfgang called him) with no dramatic experience or musical instinct. Wolfgang coached him tirelessly.

By December it was finished, and both Leopold and Nannerl went to Munich two days after Mozart's twenty-fifth birthday for the premiere of his ninth opera — *Idomeneo, King of Crete* (K. 366) — his first mature masterpiece in the form.

The story is based on a familiar legend, the same tale as that of the biblical Jephthah. On his way home to Crete after the Trojan War, Idomeneo is caught in a violent storm at sea. He rashly vows that if he reaches land safely he will sacrifice the first living thing he sees to Neptune, the sea god. Of course the first person he sees is his beloved only son, Idamante. Horrified, Idomeneo rejects his son and tries to get him to leave Crete (without telling him why). Meanwhile Idamante has problems of his own: he is in the middle of a love triangle. Two women love him, one of whom, the Trojan princess Ilia, he loves in return; the other Elettra, he doesn't. At the climax, Idomeneo is ready to sacrifice his son, but at the last minute the voice of Neptune stops him. Idomeneo abdicates in favor of Idamante and Ilia, and everyone (except Elettra) rejoices.

Idomeneo was Mozart's most ambitious work thus far, and a completely absorbing experience. The conception is large scale, with gorgeous orchestration, huge choral finales to each act, and tremendous dramatic sweep. For three hours a consistent tone is maintained: noble, strong, thrilling. For the first time the supernatural enters Mozart's music; maybe he knew there was something supernatural about himself. He became infatuated with the eerie and the terrifying. *Idomeneo* boasts two major storms, a near shipwreck (a duet for two choruses, one of horrified spectators on stage and the other of scared sailors off stage), a rampaging sea monster, a moving statue, and an oracular subterranean voice; all are set to music which heightens the unearthly situations. Wolfgang imported trumpet and trombone mutes from Salzburg for moments of dramatic solemnity.

The arias, too, are wonderful, and more than that: each character has a distinct musical personality. Particularly impressive is Elettra, who is fury incarnate, raging about the stage screaming out her frustrations.

Like all Mozart's great operas — like all his music, maybe like all music — *Idomeneo* is about love: its enormous power, how it makes life worth living, how it makes people act nobly to one another, how lack of it makes people crazy. At the heart of the story is, appropriately enough, the love between father and son. When Idamante finally learns why his father has been coldly avoiding him, he is overjoyed—he realizes how deeply his father loves him. He goes to his sacrifice willingly. Ilia's readiness to die in place of (or alongside of) her lover is the powerful magic that evoke's Neptune's pity and ensures a happy ending (although the altar gets pretty crowded with all the potential victims tripping over each other). From a rather stilted plot, Mozart refined a real story with glorious music.

Idomeneo was repeated twice and then dropped. Wolfgang heard it once more at a private concert in Vienna six years later; it was a particular favorite of his, and many of its best features return in *Don Giovanni* and *The Magic Flute*. It has never been widely performed, despite its many wonders; its first American performance was in 1947, at Tanglewood.

"The applause of a single human being is of great importance," Samuel Johnson wrote in 1781.

The elector of Bavaria was pleased, and he told Wolfgang he was amazed that "such great things were tucked away in so small a head." But neither a new commission nor a job offer came his way. Wolfgang lingered in Munich, enjoying the carnival and composing two beautiful chamber works: the Quartet for Oboe, Violin, Viola, and Cello (K. 370) and the Serenade no. 10 for Thirteen Wind Instruments (K. 361). The serenade lasts almost an hour, and even without strings it sounds full and rich, never like music for a marching band. Mozart's knowledge of each instrument is so sure, and his ability to set groups of woodwinds off against each other so sophisticated, that interest never flags. It is an extremely sensuous-sounding work, particularly in its slow movement, an adagio of expansive melodies in which the woodwinds' sustained tones sound very much like human voices. The clarinets are especially wonderful; Mozart had a special feeling for a low-register clarinet called the basset horn. In homage to this love, Bernard Shaw, writing music criticism for a London newspaper a century later, signed his reviews "Corno di Bassetto."

Wolfgang's vacation ended when Prince-Archbishop Colloredo summoned him to Vienna, where the death of Maria Theresa occasioned various solemnities. Early in March 1781, Wolfgang said goodbye to his father, who returned to Salzburg, and headed for Vienna, the city where he settled for the last ten years of his life, composing his greatest works.

What started as a routine trip turned into the double turning point of Mozart's life, from which he emerged his own man at last, personally and artistically.

II

The Last Golden Decade

4.

Set Me Free

The passionate, concentrated love of music in a great musician may be likened in its intensity to personal love.
—W.J. Turner

If Wolfgang Mozart had died at twenty-five in 1781, his place in history would nonetheless have been assured: his early symphonies, concertos, and operas are enduringly beautiful and expressive. But he lived an additional ten years; a short period, yet enough time for him to compose his richest musical statements, the pieces which plunge to the deepest abyss and soar to the highest peak of human feeling.

Mozart was bitter when he arrived in Vienna. The mastery of *Idomeneo* had not altered his status one bit; if anything, the prince-archbishop's resentment and hostility increased because of it. Two mutually exclusive attitudes met head on: Mozart saw himself as a genius, Colloredo saw him as a servant. Mozart had been honored by kings, emperors, and the pope, and he had been told by outstanding musicians and music lovers all over Europe that genius like his appears once in a century. He was bursting to break free of the restrictions of the Salzburg court and its overbearing rules. Perhaps in the back of his mind he realized that the time had come to break his father's stranglehold as well.

Colloredo intensified his humiliation of the composer. Mozart lived in the archbishop's quarters under supervision; he ate with the cook, valet, and other servants, whom Mozart disdained as much as he was disdained by the archbishop. The archbishop addressed him in language reserved for children or the most menial servants. Mozart was subjected to all kinds of rudeness; he particularly objected to having to wait in the unheated foyers of rich people's homes until it was time to perform, lest he mingle with the nobles chatting lazily inside. (In the 1920s a story went around that a wealthy woman asked a famous violinist to appear at one of her parties. He said he would play for five thousand dollars. The host reluctantly agreed, and quickly added that the maestro was not to mix with the guests. "In that case, three thousand dollars," he said.)

Vienna in Mozart's time.

Worst of all for Mozart, he was forbidden to play at concerts unless the archbishop gave his permission, nor could he independently seek any musical engagements or commissions to supplement his small salary. "It is perfectly true that his vanity is tickled by possessing my person," he wrote his father, "but what use is all that to me? One cannot live on it." Mozart's anger flared when the archbishop denied him permission to perform at a large public concert for the benefit of musicians' widows after he had announced he would play. All musical Vienna would be there, and Mozart was eager for everyone to hear his newest works. Under pressure from some of the composer's more influential fans, Colloredo relented, but Mozart's triumph at the concert only made the archbishop more determined to put Mozart in what he thought was his place. He forbade absolutely any more concerts. "His lordship the archbishop has the goodness to glory in his people—to rob them of their chances to earn money—and not to pay them for it," complained Mozart to his father. Leopold advised patience and restraint.

An eighteenth-century concert.

But the "most obedient son" had been pushed too far by the "archfool." His insults had stuck. Mozart was proud and sensitive, unable to slough off rudeness and abuse from anyone, let alone be treated like an object.

In the beginning of May, the prince-archbishop and his retinue packed up for the return to Salzburg. Mozart was eager to remain in the capital, where he had become quite popular. Colloredo not only insisted that Mozart return with him, but through a messenger handed Mozart "an important parcel" for him to carry back. The meaning was clear. Mozart refused, moved out of the archbishop's quarters, and announced his intention of staying in Vienna another week. Colloredo, furious, sent for him.

Only Mozart's version of what happened next exists, in his letters to his father; however exaggerated it may be, it has the ring of truth. Colloredo screamed at him nonstop, the composer finding it "impossible to get a word in." The archbishop called him a knave, a slovenly rascal, a conceited scoundrel, a vagabond. Finally

Mozart broke in sarcastically: "So your grace is not satisfied with me?" "What, you dare to threaten me, you idiot! There is the door! I will have no more to do with such a miserable wretch!" "Nor I with you!" answered the ex-servant, and stomped out. He was in a state, "feverish, trembling in every limb, staggering across the street like a drunkard."

It was Mozart's first act of disobedience to the establishment.

More humiliation was in store for Mozart. When he returned to the archbishop's with his formal resignation, Colloredo refused to see him. Instead the archbishop's steward told Mozart that he needed his father's permission to quit. Mozart returned a second time and again his resignation was refused. On his third attempt he got into a raging argument with the steward, who then "hurled me out of the room with a kick on my ass" and into the street. Mozart vowed vengeance in kind. As it turned out, he never saw Colloredo or his steward again, but no matter: he had his revenge in living well and composing his way to immortality.

Even crueler than the kick was Leopold's reaction. Mozart begged his father to support him in his resolve to break free; "my honor, as you know, is above everything precious to me." Instead Leopold urged Mozart to humble himself and seek a reconciliation, suggesting that his son had jeopardized Leopold's position with the archbishop as well. Mozart stood firm: "Do trust me always, for indeed I deserve it."

Leopold took his son's perseverance badly, and he let loose a nightmarish torrent: Mozart had never shown him any affection or loyalty at all and should show some now for the first time, he wrote bitterly.

"Can you really say this?" asked Mozart, stunned and horrified. "I must confesss there is not a single trait in your letter by which I could have recognized my father!" Having defied his boss, Mozart now went against his father's wishes for the first time in twenty-five years. Once liberation begins, there's no telling where, if at all, it will end. A new life had started.

Unlike the dutiful Nannerl, Mozart stopped saving his father's letters, or perhaps just carelessly lost them, from 1781 onward. He had plenty to do, and "it does not help me in the very least to read unpleasant letters," he wrote Leopold.

Mozart's boldness was strengthened by his enthusiastic reception in Vienna—"pianoland" as he called it—and by a new commission from Emperor Joseph II to write a German opera for Vienna's National Theater. In the eighteenth century, Germany was a figment of the imagination; it was politically divided, and culturally enslaved by French and Italian models. A national theater was an idea that Mozart was eager to make a reality. "How much more popular I should be if I could help forward the German national theater," Mozart had written from Munich in 1777.

Not that there was anything mystically German about German opera, the operetta form in which Mozart first composed when he was twelve. Its musical antecedents were as much French and Italian as they were German, except for the simple folksonglike tunes often used. But it was sung and spoken in German at a time when the courts and gentry spoke French. Previous settings of German words to music of the German people—the chorale settings of Johann Sebastian Bach are the finest—were generally unknown.

No one, not even a genius, is Everyman. Mozart was a German-speaking Austrian of the late eighteenth century, and his musical concerns reflect it. But his music also transcends his personal background: time and place slither away as the magic of his melodies and harmonies fills a room.

And there was one more source of Mozart's new-found courage. When he left the archbishop's house he had to find a place to live, and who should be renting rooms but old Mrs. Weber, Aloysia's mother. Mozart was "still not indifferent" to Aloysia Lange, nor she to him, but her husband was "a jealous fool who never lets her out of his sight." Her younger sister, eighteen-year-old Constanze, became his heart's desire. She, too, was musical, both a singer and a pianist. Mozart gave her lessons. He must have liked the way she played.

Mrs. Weber watched over the growing romance between her daughter and boarder with avid interest, eager to marry off yet another of her four girls. She helped spread the rumor that Mozart and Constanze were engaged, and the rumor reached as far as Salzburg. Leopold, who thought no woman good enough for his Wolfgang, fumed and thundered. Mozart, still under Leopold's influence, moved out of the Webers' house.

That summer Mozart was handed the libretto of his German opera, a revision of an old French romance now called *The Abduction from the Seraglio*. By chance the leading female character was named Constanze. No doubt pleased by this happy omen, Mozart worked on the score with a full heart.

To make money he gave lessons, and as a well-known pianist he soon had plenty of pupils. One of the first, Josephine von Aurnhammer, fell madly in love with him. She was a fine pianist, and Mozart wrote his virtuosic and spirited Sonata for Two Pianos (K. 448) for the two of them. Although piano duets—one piano, four hands—were not uncommon, the use of two pianos was. The greatly increased sonority resulted in a lush, almost symphonic effect. Josephine was enormously fat and ugly; "one is punished enough for the rest of the day if by sad misfortune one has cast an eye on her," the ungallant Mozart wrote. Constanze Weber was looking better and better.

As Mozart worked on his love-drenched libretto, his passion for Constanze simmered. By December 1781, he broke the news to Leopold, having previously denied strenuously any romantic affiliations. "She is not ugly, although anything but beautiful," the honest lover wrote. "Her whole beauty consists in two small, black eyes, and a handsome figure. She has not wit, but enough sound human sense to be able to fulfill her duties as a wife and mother."

If Mozart seemed less than head-over-heels in love, he was neverthelesss extremely eager to get married, and not just because rumor was forcing him. Nearly twenty-six and by nature flirtatious and romantic, he was probably still a virgin. He'd been tempted often enough, but his strict morality had stopped him. "I am too honorable to seduce an innocent girl, and have too much horror and disgust, too much fear and loathing of disease, to go with whores," he wrote, a not-unwise stance in the days before penicillin. As a child, Mozart had always craved love and affection. Now, cut off from his family and bitter at Leopold's criticisms, he wanted love more than ever, including the sexual kind. "The voice of nature speaks as loud in me as in others, louder, perhaps, than in many a big strong lout of a fellow" was Mozart's discreet way of putting it.

And Mozart was incapable of living a comfortable life alone. He had always had his mundane needs met by servants, mother, and sister. He was too full of musical ideas to take much notice of clean clothes, although he liked to be well-dressed.

Most of all, Mozart wanted a haven, a home with warmth and love, a respite from the tiring round of concerts and lessons. His profession was in some ways a lonely one, and his genius made it lonelier, cutting him off from other musicians whose work Mozart didn't respect. He didn't want a lonely personal life was well.

Constanze loved him. "She has the kindest heart in the world, and—I love her and she me with all our hearts! Could I wish myself a better wife?" No indeed. All the music in the world, however full of emotion, is no substitute for the real thing.

Mozart knew his father's objections: Constanze was poorly educated and came from a not-too-respectable family connected with the theater. Maybe his father's attitude only made the match sweeter to Mozart, as a final gesture of independence and adulthood. Mozart had had enough of being treated like a child.

The decisive stroke came late in December. At Mrs. Weber's urging, Mozart signed a contract to protect Constanze's compromised reputation. Mozart promised to either marry her within three years or pay her an annual stipend for life (apparently Aloysia's engagement had had the same romantic beginning). The "angelic girl" took the document from her mother and tore it up, telling Mozart that "I need no written assurance from you. I believe what you say." A far stronger commitment existed by then; it was just a matter of time.

Mozart's work on his opera occupied him steadily. His patron, the emperor, interrupted him with a demand to provide entertainment for the visit to Vienna of Catherine the Great's son, Grand Duke Paul of Russia ("the big noise," Mozart called him). The emperor set up a piano duel between Mozart and Muzio Clementi, a famous composer and piano virtuoso. The two pianists took turns playing difficult pieces, improvising on the other's themes, and in general striving to outshine each other. Clementi mistook Mozart for a valet because of his elegant clothes, getting the festivities off to a fine start. Mozart was unimpressed with Clementi: "he has nothing, not the least interpretation or taste, much less feeling." Years later, he borrowed a theme from one of Clementi's works he had heard at the duel for his overture to *The Magic Flute*; such unconscious tune-snatching happens frequently.

Piano duels became a fixture of nineteenth-century musical life, and the principle continues in the form of piano competitions. When artists compete, who wins?

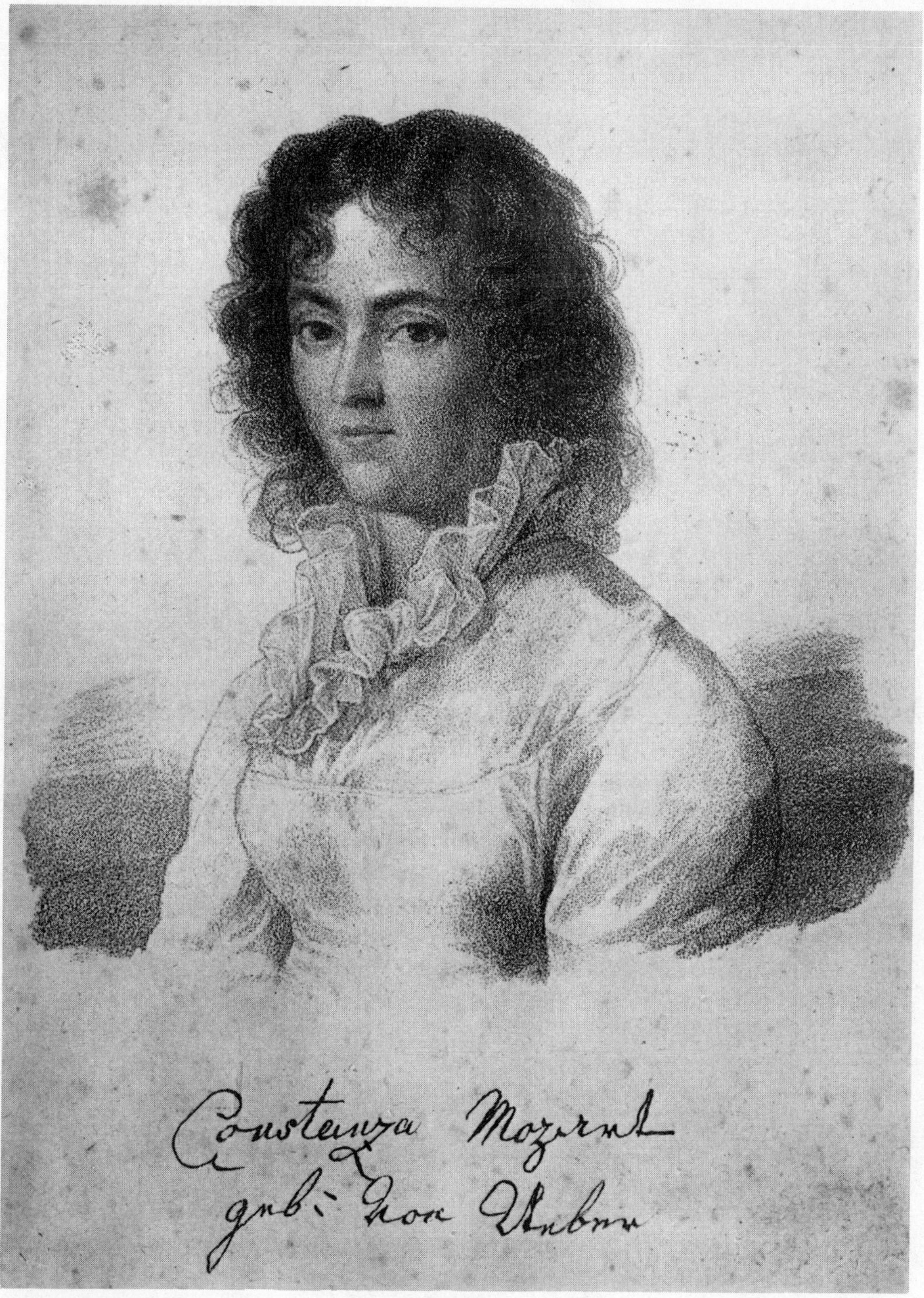

Constanze Mozart.

AUSTRIAN INFORMATION SERVICE

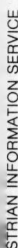

Joseph Haydn.

In December, Mozart met the composer whose music he most esteemed: Joseph Haydn. The son of peasants, Haydn was in the service of Prince Esterházy in Hungary. He remained with the Esterházys, one of Europe's wealthiest families, for thirty years; in 1790 he wrote, "it is indeed sad to be always a slave."

Although Prince Esterházy frequently restricted Haydn's freedom to travel, Haydn's music had traveled as far as England and Russia. Mozart had heard Haydn symphonies in Vienna as early as 1773, and he admired their power and brilliance. Haydn virtually invented the string quartet, and by the 1780s he had already written forty, many of which Mozart knew from scores. Soon after their first meeting, Mozart began a string quartet, one of the few pieces he ever wrote without financial motivation. The meeting proved to be the beginning of a beautiful friendship, whose only flaw was how little time the two had to spend together.

In March 1782, Mozart made his first public appearance in Vienna as a free agent. He conducted his own music, doubling as soloist in a piano concerto. Later concerts were given in a large open-air setting in a Viennese park, next to a fashionable restaurant.

By then his new opera was finished, held up by disagreements with the librettist even more extensive than those over *Idomeneo*. The official opening was also delayed because of intrigues against Mozart. Other musicians tended to be envious of his achievement and put off by his self-confidence and intolerance of much of their music. There were paid boo-ers in the packed house—but no Leopold—when *The Abduction from the Seraglio* (K. 384) opened in July.

The story is simple enough. Constanze and her maid, Blonde, are captives of Pasha Selim. Selim is in love with Constanze, and his servant Osmin wants Blonde. Belmonte, Constanze's lover, gains entry to the palace by pretending to be an architect, and, with the help of his servant, Pedrillo (who is naturally Blonde's lover), plans an escape. The four are caught by Osmin, but Selim magnanimously lets them go, and everyone (except Osmin) rejoices.

Dramatically, Mozart chose to emphasize two themes: love and honor. Love shows up in many guises. Constanze, as her name implies, is faithfulness itself. She won't give in to Selim's first, gentle suggestions, and the exasperated pasha then threatens. She replies with an enormous aria, passionate and heroic, that she will endure "tortures of all kinds" rather than betray Belmonte. If she can sing the aria well, she doubtless has the strength to endure plenty. Nothing like this aria had ever been heard in German-language music theaters before.

Belmonte, the lovesick hero, is a part Mozart clearly understood. Mozart's favorite aria was Belmonte's "Oh, What Anguish," and he described to his father the way his music fit the words: "You feel the trembling—the faltering—you see how his throbbing breast begins to swell; this I have expressed by a crescendo. You hear the whispering and the sighing—which I have indicated by the first violins with mutes and a flute playing in unison." Two violins playing the same note an octave apart represented the heartthrob. The music goes beyond the decorative into the expressive.

For some reason Blonde is English, and she fends off Osmin by telling him she is "born to freedom" and not to be pushed around. Women are not chattel, and, as if to prove it, the women are provided the most compelling tunes.

As the rescue is about to begin, Belmonte admits his doubts about Constanze's fidelity, and Constanze is ready to stop the escape right then. Love means treating people a certain way—in this case, trustingly. Her point made, she allows the rescue to continue. All of this takes place in a light, humorous manner; the opera contains plenty of sight gags and a hilarious drunk scene. But real ideas and emotions are involved.

The ending is unexpectedly profound: when the lovers are captured, Selim finds out that Belmonte is the son of his worst enemy, the man who drove him from his homeland. The lovers sing a sad farewell to life when Selim interrupts them. "I dislike your father too much to follow in his footsteps. Tell him it gave me far greater pleasure to reward an injustice with justice." This nobility of character is the opera's climax.

Mozart knew all about nobility: the literal kind, the "Princess Dunghills" he had to entertain, and the real kind. Honor was the issue with Colloredo, with Leopold, with his own Constanze.

Framed with choruses in his most exotic "Turkish" style—the liveliest and most colorful music Mozart had yet written—*Abduction from the Seraglio* was a sensational success. The imperial family led the roof-shattering applause; so many arias were encored that the evening lasted six hours. It was quickly taken up in German-language opera houses from Prague to Frankfurt, and became, as Mozart had hoped, the cornerstone of German opera, the first in a proud line that climaxed in 1935 with Alban Berg's *Lulu*.

Emperor Joseph's remark at the end of the performance is a jewel of insightful criticism: "Too beautiful for our ears, my dear Mozart, and an extraordinary number of notes." Mozart is said to have answered "exactly as many as are needed"; what could he have thought about such shallowness?

The opera's many performances that season were gratifying, but did nothing to help Mozart financially: a theater paid a flat fee for an opera, and there were no royalties. The only way to make more money was to sell the score to another theater or arrange the music for piano and sell the score to amateurs. In either case the absence of copyright meant that anyone who got the full score or made a piano reduction could sell Mozart's music without paying the composer at all. In the case of *Abduction*, Mozart was almost halfway through a piano score when he learned someone else had beat him to it. Nor were authors protected; later that year the playwright whose play was the source of *Abduction*'s libretto ran an ad in a Leipzig newspaper to inform everyone that "a certain Mozart in Vienna has had the impudence to misuse my drama as the text of an opera."

As he often did, Mozart followed an opera with an orchestral work in the same spirit. In July 1782, the Haffners of Salzburg commissioned another serenade. That work is lost, but later Mozart arranged four of its six movements as a symphony. The *Haffner* Symphony, no. 35 (K. 385) "positively amazed me," Mozart wrote his father, "for I had forgotten every single note of it." Written in haste, the symphony is amazing: its slow movement sings a sensuous song of love, perhaps inspired by Constanze. Mozart's outdoor concerts generally ended just after dark; the finale of the *Haffner* Symphony, marked "as fast as possible," is ideal music by which to watch the stars come out.

Mozart's love affair climaxed that summer. Her mother's torments had led Constanze to run off to a friend's house, and Mrs. Weber threatened to call the police. Mozart dashed off a letter to Leopold asking his blessing, and without waiting for a reply set the date. On August 4, 1782, Mozart and Constanze were married. The following day Mozart received Leopold's grudging blessings.

Their marriage was happy. They stayed in love with each other, as Mozart's affectionate and sexy letters to his wife reveal. Constanze became pregnant at once, and with rare exception remained so throughout her eight years of marriage. She was no great intellect and enjoyed partying, but she was by no means the ignorant slut that some later Mozart-worshippers described.

As an object of near-veneration for two centuries, Mozart was assumed to have married "beneath" him. In his own lifetime, Viennese gossips claimed the ever affectionate composer had affairs with all his pupils, leading ladies, chambermaids, and whoever else caught his eye. His early death was attributed to these "excesses" and even to venereal disease; there is, however, no evidence that Mozart contracted the disease which would have killed Schubert—had not that unlucky composer succumbed to typhoid fever first, at the age of thirty-one. The most lurid Mozart scandal occurred just after his death. Franz Hofdemel, one of Mozart's friends and creditors, attacked his own wife with a razor and then killed himself, apparently in a fit of jealousy. Magdalena Hofdemel, who had been a piano student of Mozart's, lived and gave birth to a son a few months later. She named the boy Johann, one of Mozart's names but also the commonest German given name.

In any case, Mozart and Constanze were happy. Maybe she didn't appreciate the full depths of his genius, but few people then did. But she loved music and his in particular, found it special, and did everything she could to encourage him in his work, no small virtue.

The young couple lived on the money Mozart made teaching piano and playing his works at concerts. His busy schedule included intimate Sunday-morning concerts at his home, a three-room apartment in a crowded section of inner-city Vienna. With no fixed income, the Mozarts could not afford luxury.

Among Mozart's admirers was Baron van Swieten, a music lover whose mansion was the scene of weekly chamber-music concerts. Van Swieten became something of a patron to Mozart for the rest of his life; he also helped Beethoven, who dedicated his First Symphony to him in 1800. Van Swieten's musical library was vast and his knowledge extensive. Drawing upon both, he introduced Mozart to the music of Johann Sebastian Bach. The impact was electric, genius to genius. Mozart knew of Bach through his famous sons, and he had learned counterpoint as a child. But the magnificent fugues of the *Well-tempered Clavier* and the *Art of the Fugue* were a revelation, as the most complex musical forms merged with the deepest expressivity. Mozart arranged some of Bach's fugues for string quartet and added his own

One of Mozart's Vienna homes.

preludes (K. 404a), producing an extraordinary collaboration full of contrasts and sympathies. Constanze Mozart loved fugues, and she encouraged Mozart to use them more often. He did, adding to his exceptional melodic abundance and rich harmonic color.

All of Mozart's music for solo instruments other than those he played—piano, violin, and viola—were written for particular players. Late in 1782, he wrote a Horn Quintet (K. 407) and the first of four Horn Concertos (K. 412, K. 417, K. 447, K. 495) for Ignaz Leutgeb, the leading horn virtuoso of his day. His instrument, a forerunner of the French horn, had no valves, and the player changed the size of the opening with his hand to get (or approximate) the desired note. Leutgeb struck Mozart's fancy for some reason; perhaps because his great skill existed in an artistic vacuum. Leutgeb soon stopped playing and opened a cheese store. The scores of these concertos are covered with Mozart's personal notes to Leutgeb, their dedicatee and "ass, ox, and fool": "Now, you ass, play for your life! Well done! Courage! You pig!" In the fourth concerto, Mozart wrote out the solo part in four colors just to make it more confusing. The solo parts in all the concertos are elaborate and intricate, contrasting sharply with the instrument's heavy, reverberant tone. They are like hunt music for catching unusually agile elephants.

The letters between Mozart and his father had grown less frequent and less affectionate since Mozart's double independence of 1781. The two hadn't seen each other since, and Mozart was eager for his father and sister to meet Constanze. Naturally Leopold expected to be visited, but the Mozarts' trip to Salzburg had to be delayed because of Mozart's concert schedule and Constanze's pregnancy. Mozart had asked Leopold to be godfather, with the assumption that the child would be named after him. But when a boy was born in June he was named Raimund Leopold, Mozart's father being upstaged by Mozart's landlord, a subtle statement. Mozart worked on a string quartet (K. 421) while Constanze was in labor, and he reputedly finished the minuet movement during the delivery. He was famous for being able to compose under any circumstances, weaving in and out of his personal creative world to talk, drink, or play billiards (his favorite game) while composing.

Mozart and Constanze left for Salzburg at the end of July. It was considered vulgar for a genteel mother to nurse her child, and month-old Raimund, "a fine sturdy boy as round as a ball," was given to a wet nurse. The visit lasted four months, but it was not what Mozart had hoped: both Leopold and Nannerl were cool and not at all taken with Constanze. In his childhood, Mozart could do no wrong in his adoring father's eyes, and now that blissful state was only a sweet memory.

Mozart brought with him an unfinished mass, his first church music since leaving the archbishop (who, Leopold feared, would arrest the ex-servant). It was an uncommissioned work in fulfillment of a vow Mozart made if Constanze recovered from an illness. As a Catholic he took his vow seriously, but despite much free time in Salzburg he didn't finish the mass; it remained incomplete, as did all the music he wrote for his wife. But what is there is almost an hour of Mozart's most glorious vocal music, in a wide range of styles: opera arias, modern orchestral harmonies, and an eight-part double fugue showing Bach's influence. A combination of deepest sincerity and secular glitter, the stylistic inconsistencies of the work do not matter compared to its overall opulence. Constanze sang one of the soprano parts when the "Great" Mass (K. 427) was performed in Salzburg that August; if she were not an exceptional singer, she must have made a mess of the beautiful and difficult role.

They left Salzburg at the end of October. Mozart never returned to his hometown and never again saw his sister.

On their way home they stopped in Linz—the Austrian town which has lent its name to a large jelly-filled cookie—to visit the father-in-law of one of Mozart's pupils. Count Thun wanted a symphony for a concert he was giving in a few days, and Mozart wrote Leopold, "as I don't have a single symphony with me, I am writing a new one at breakneck speed." The *Linz* Symphony, no. 36 (K. 425), shows Haydn's influence, from the slow introduction preceding the fast first movement to the peasant-dance minuet. But no matter who influenced Mozart—Christian Bach, Gluck, Haydn—the music always came out with that recognizably personal sound which made the word *Mozartean* necessary.

For the same concert, Mozart wrote an introduction to a symphony by Michael Haydn, Joseph's younger brother and a Salzburg friend of the family. The entire symphony was later assumed to be by Mozart and was assigned all the identification: no. 37, K. 444. The later symphonies had become well-known by the time Michael Haydn's authorship was discovered, and they were not renumbered. Mozart's symphonies now progress directly from no. 36 to no. 38.

In 1783, the United States was recognized by Great Britain.

When they returned to Vienna, Mozart and Constanze learned that Raimund had died while they had been in Salzburg.

Mozart composed vigorously: another string quartet, sketches for an Italian opera that was never completed. Sometime in his early Vienna stay he composed a strange little work, an unfinished Piano Fantasy (K. 397), improvisatory in style, spooky in sound. It begins with an eerie melody that could have come from a music box in a bad dream, and ends with the most frivolous allegro, almost a self-parody. In its own small way, this piece contains the extremes of Mozart's emotional style: the somber, even weird, tones of some unnamed restlessness along with the pretty, polished, and eternally carefree.

After 1783, the emotions in Mozart's music are increasingly contradictory, and it becomes more and more difficult to tell whether a given piece is predominantly happy or sad. There is, however, no controversy about the music's extraordinary beauty or technical mastery.

5.

What Price Glory?

All these people flew about in sheer delight to my music.
—Mozart, 1787

In February 1784, Mozart began keeping a thematic catalogue of his works. Aside from easing the work of future cataloguers, his musical diary indicates a new attitude toward his compositions. No eighteenth-century composer consciously wrote for posterity, but Mozart wanted a record of everything he created.

Underneath the shimmering melodies lies an audible sense of gloom, doom, and melancholy shot through with nostalgia. For what? His superstar childhood? Leopold's love? Or is it the awareness that life is like that, emotionally ambiguous. "In the greatest happiness there is always something lacking," he wrote.

There was plenty of happiness and glory in Vienna, where Mozart's friends included artists and intellectuals as well as the usual rich music lovers. His concerts were very well attended, and although his renown stemmed mostly from his playing, the music he played was always his own. His specialty was the piano concerto, and he began the year by composing six new ones, nos. 14–19 (K. 449, K. 450, K. 451, K 453, K. 456, K. 459), all but one for his own use, in rapid succession. Like all his twenty-seven concertos, these last about twenty minutes (conveniently one LP record side) and follow the fast-slow-fast pattern. Each is special in its own way; no. 17 is especially lovely, and the folksonglike theme in its last movement was inspired by a tune whistled by Mozart's pet starling. No. 18 was written for a twenty-five-year-old blind pianist, Maria Theresa Paradis, who was also a composer; no. 19 boasts the largest finale, a complex synthesis of operatic melodies and fugue that perfectly crowns the series.

He found time to complete another string quartet, no. 17 (K. 458), later subtitled "The Hunt" because of a hunting-horn theme in its first movement. At this time Mozart decided to dedicate a series of his string quartets to Haydn, whose long stay in Vienna had strengthened their friendship. The rise of Haydn's importance to Mozart correlates directly with the fall of Leopold's. Haydn was twenty-four years older than Mozart, practically Leopold's age; to make it even better, his nickname was "Papa." The two friends played each other's string quartets at Mozart's home, Haydn on first violin, Mozart on viola.

In August 1784, Nannerl Mozart, then thirty-three, married the much older Baron Berchtold zu Sonnenberg, a widower with five children. It was said to have been a marriage of convenience after Nannerl was jilted by an army officer.

Mozart finished the year with a Quintet for Piano and Wind Instruments (K. 452) which "is the best which I have yet written in my life." In September his second son, Karl Thomas, was born. He lived to seventy-four, dying in 1858. He became a talented pianist but soon gave up music as a profession. He lived in Italy on a beautiful estate bought with a small share of his father's by then considerable royalties. He never married.

Among the more progressive in Mozart's circles were those who were Freemasons, and Mozart joined the order at the end of 1784. Freemasonry was a near-comprehensive compendium of the highest ideals of the time, taking the optimistic view of human perfectability through struggle and love. In more than two hundred years these ideals have not lost their unique power to move people—just like Mozart's music. Originally stone cutters' guilds, masonic lodges used the symbolism of building to express a philosophy and morality stressing benevolence and the acceptance of death. Its imagery and architecture were saturated with orientalism, with a vaguely Egyptian flavor.

Mozart's attraction to Freemasonry was immediate and intense, especially since its ideas coincided with many of his own. Genius and teacher, he needed to be taught as well. Because of its secret oath, anticlerical and in general liberal politics, and its religious tolerance (even Jews could join), Freemasonry was condemned by the Catholic Church in 1738, and any Catholic who became a Mason was in danger of excommunication. Bolder and bolder, Mozart joined the Benevolence Lodge while remaining a Catholic. In a way Freemasonry supplanted religion the way Haydn had supplanted Leopold. Its hold on Mozart remained strong for the rest of his life.

Mozart began 1785 by composing two more string quartets, no. 18 (K. 464) and, four days later, no. 19 (K. 465); together the String Quartets nos. 14–19 are called the *Haydn* Quartets because Mozart dedicated them to "his best friend." Much confusion has resulted when a piece of music is identified verbally by what sounds like "Mozart-Haydn-quartet." The last one is called "Dissonance" because it opens with a slow, chromatic section that sounds more like Mahler than Mozart. The engraver returned this quartet to its composer because of its "obvious mistakes." A Hungarian aristocrat accused his musicians of playing incorrectly when they performed it, and when shown the score he tore it to pieces. Haydn said simply, "if Mozart wrote thus, he must have done so with good reason."

(Mozart was not the last composer to have scores corrected by editors and publishers, resulting in significant variations in printed scores. It was widely

Symbols of Freemasonry: architecture, astrology, the number three.

assumed that the many difficulties in Beethoven's extraordinary late quartets were a result of his deafness, and therefore they were "corrected." Charles Ives wrote to his publisher at the beginning of the twentieth century, "Please do not change the wrong notes. They are right.")

Mozart's dedication is extremely loving: "I send my six sons to you . . . please receive them kindly . . . and maintain your generous friendship to someone who appreciates it so much." Uncommissioned, and the result, unusual for Mozart to admit, of "long and laborious toil," the *Haydn* Quartets are serious but by no means grim music, a perfect tribute to a friendship. Among the rivalries and intrigues of Vienna, the mutual admiration and affection of Mozart and Haydn seem all the purer.

Certainly Haydn had no reason to feel threatened by Mozart, for his own genius was unquestioned. Music history has echoed Mozart's personal opinion that only he and Haydn were writing really exceptional music. Haydn's most popular works, his last twelve symphonies, were written in London just after Mozart's death, when Haydn's patron's death left him a free agent. Although Haydn shared a similar musical vocabulary, style, and esthetic with Mozart, their music is not easily confused after a few hearings. Neither is better: Mozart's music tends to be more chromatic, more tender or affectionate (what used to be called "feminine"), and more disturbing than Haydn's vigorous, often wholly cheerful music.

In February 1785, Leopold Mozart visited his son, daughter-in-law, and grandchild in Vienna, and his three-month stay proved wonderful. While he was there he met Haydn, who had come to play (and thereby hear) the quartets Mozart had dedicated to him. As Leopold reported to Nannerl, Haydn turned to him and said, "I tell you before God, and I am an honest man, that your son is the greatest composer I know, either personally or by name; he has taste and the greatest science in composition." All that, and an unnameable magic.

Leopold had other reasons to be proud. After helping his son carry his fortepiano (with an added-on, knee-operated set of pedals, its "white" keys black and the sharps and flats white) from home to the concert hall, he heard him play and conduct his Piano Concerto no. 20 (K. 466), one of the greatest works in the form. Its shuddering beginning and dark, passionate energy make it clear why Mozart's contemporaries and immediate successors thought of him as the first romantic composer. Full of pathos and soul-searching, this concerto was Beethoven's favorite; he played it, wrote cadenzas for it, and used it as a model for his own five piano concertos. It was one of the handful of orchestral works by which Mozart was known throughout the nineteenth and well into the twentieth century, a work which in large part defined that element of Mozart's music called "demonic."

A month later Mozart introduced his Piano Concerto no. 21 (K. 467), now his most widely known piece of music (or section of one): its slow movement was used as part of the sound track for the film *Elvira Madigan* and, arranged for hundreds of strings, has gone around the world many times in elevators and various public spaces. Less turbulent and more peaceful than its predecessor, this concerto's yearning, sadly sweet, singing slow movement fully deserves its enormous popularity.

Leopold had to admit that his son was doing fine without him (even financially), and he even joined his son's Masonic lodge as a loving gesture. Neither Leopold nor Haydn, who also became a Mason under Mozart's urging, participated in lodge life.

Leopold Mozart left Vienna in April 1785. It was the last time that father and son saw each other.

Mozart returned to writing piano sonatas for the first time in seven years. In May he wrote a fantasy which he attached to a sonata in the same key. The combined Piano Fantasy-Sonata (K. 475–K. 457) is the longest work for solo piano before Beethoven's mature sonatas. Improvising had been Mozart's most impressive feat since he was six, and the fantasy form gives some indication of his rich musical imagination. It is always a thrill when a performer appears to be composing the piece while he or she is playing it; Keith Jarrett's work is a good contemporary example. And improvising gives a sharp insight into composing—the two can be synonymous.

As one of the stars of Vienna, Mozart did not live a life of all work and no play. He had a billiard table installed in his apartment and played often, composing all the while. His musical ability to plan moves ahead might have made him a good player, but a pianist's fingers are accustomed to arching, hardly conducive to wielding a cue stick. He loved parties, with their opportunity to flirt, and he often joked that he was a better dancer than composer. His favorite parties were costume affairs; he asked Leopold to send him a harlequin costume for a party that "began at six and ended at seven. What? Only an hour? Of course not, from six in the evening to seven next morning." He liked to drink — "punch" or beer, not whiskey — and not to drunkenness, just enough to get high.

In July 1785 Nannerl's first child was born. Not one to take chances, she named the boy Leopold. The child lived with his namesake for the next two years.

At first Mozart was not "misunderstood" or neglected in Vienna, only badly payed. He taught in the mornings and early afternoons, performed in the evenings, and composed (mostly at the piano) at night, since childhood his preferred time for creative activity. Money was coming in, but the Mozarts were soon in debt, and they remained so. Neither of them was extravagant or wasteful, but both liked to live well and neither knew how to budget or cared to learn. They were pioneers in what soon came to be a middle-class tradition—living beyond their means. They never starved and always employed at least one maid, but they frequently didn't have the rent money.

Mozart demonstrated his commitment to Freemasonry by writing music for various Masonic events. In November 1785, two leading lodge brothers died, and Mozart composed the Masonic Funeral Music (K. 477) in their memory. A mournful adagio written over a melody derived from a Catholic psalm, its strength and resignation make death seem a welcome release, a spiritual climax. The orchestra-

Lorenzo da Ponte.

tion is heavy with low-register woodwinds, suggesting an organ but less majestic, more intimate. Some people spend gloomy afternoons thinking about what music they'd like played at their funeral; this would do fine.

In December 1785 the *Vienna Times*, then as now one of Europe's leading newspapers, reviewed a concert in which Mozart played one of his concertos (in between the halves of someone else's oratorio). "Our praise is superfluous in view of the deserved fame of this master, as well known as he is universally valued."

High praise indeed, but again Mozart was seized with the desire to write an opera. His opportunity arrived in the person of Lorenzo da Ponte, a court poet in Vienna since 1783. Born in 1749 of Italian Jewish parents, da Ponte became in rapid succession a Catholic, a priest, a romantic adventurer, and a playwright. His long and adventurous life ended in New York City in 1838, where in his last years da Ponte was the first professor of Italian at Columbia University, founded two years before Mozart was born. Columbia still has a da Ponte chair in Italian literature.

Da Ponte had written a libretto for an opera by Antonio Salieri, then the favorite opera composer of the emperor and Viennese public. The opera failed, and Salieri blamed da Ponte. Eager to restore his reputation, da Ponte approached Mozart, who suggested using Beaumarchais's *The Marriage of Figaro*. In da Ponte's extravagant memoirs, he claimed Mozart wrote the music as fast as he wrote the words, finishing the entire score in six weeks, by March 1786.

Beaumarchais's comedy, a sequel to his lighter *Barber of Seville,* was produced in Paris after much difficulty in 1784, seven years after it was written. On the day it was to be presented in Vienna it was banned on the emperor's orders because "this piece contains much that is objectionable." As Napoleon later commented, "in that play the French Revolution had already begun." Figaro is a servant who fights back against the institutionalized stupidities and injustices of feudal society as personified by Count Almaviva, his boss. In his clearest statement on the subject, Figaro makes his point exactly: "Because you are a noble lord you think yourself a superior human being. How have you earned so many advantages? By being born. I have had to battle for mere existence with more wits, effort, and ingenuity than are used to govern Spain in a century!"

At first the emperor refused da Ponte permission to use this inflammatory play, but da Ponte promised to cut the most "objectionable" passages, including the above one. But the play's egalitarian spirit remained, if only through innuendo and its deadly accurate portrayal of the aristocracy's shallow grandeur. When Joseph II heard excerpts of the score he was "delighted, not to say astounded," and gave the necessary approval. Salieri and his clique did what they could to delay the premiere, which finally took place, appropriately enough, on May Day 1786, the composer conducting.

In essence, the plot of *The Marriage of Figaro* (K. 492) is simple. Figaro, formally a barber of Seville, is a valet of Count Almaviva. Figaro loves Susanna, Countess Almaviva's maid, and is about to marry her. The count tries to exercise the so-called seigneurial right, the traditional "right" of a feudal master to sleep with the bride of any of his vassals on her wedding night. Not officially a law, the practice was (and in modern dress is) not uncommon. To prevent him, Figaro and Susanna join forces with the countess (who was a commoner when the count first met her), who is trying to win back her husband's affections and prevent his philandering. "That's how all modern husbands are!" she laments, "systematically unfaithful, and out of vanity totally jealous." They plan to embarrass the count by a number of disguises and tricks, most involving Cherubino, a lovesick teenage boy. The final scene, in a moonlit garden, achieves this purpose and temporarily, at least, promises a happy ending for everybody (no exceptions).

As always, the theme is love; perhaps sexual politics. Because Figaro and Susanna love each other they treat each other well (except for some good-natured teasing) and work together to overcome the many obstacles to their happiness, including another woman whom Figaro promised to marry if he couldn't repay a loan,

Scene from The Marriage of Figaro *(New York City Opera): Figaro (right) and Susanna (standing) plot to*

safeguard their happiness from Count Almaviva (seated).

and who turns out to be his long-lost mother. Figaro's and Susanna's quick minds, high spirits, and tender hearts are captured from the first notes of the overture (as usual, the last part composed).

Also perfectly captured is the pain of love gone sour. "Where are they, those beautiful moments," ponders the countess in what is perhaps the most poignant melody of the opera, the same tune Mozart used in his *Coronation* Mass (K. 317) seven years earlier. It could be a typically Mozartean concerto slow movement, and here the melody is unambiguously set to words of longing for lost love and happiness. The adolescent Cherubino's music represents sexuality in its first burst; the part is written for a mezzo-soprano, the first of many great "trouser parts" in opera. Her timbre is ideally suited to an ardent youth not yet a man.

Perhaps the best parts of this incredibly fast-moving opera are its ensembles, especially the two finales (at the end of the second and fourth acts). In the first, seven protagonists sing of their various reactions to the plot in a blazing crescendo of voices and instruments, and in the second the mysteries of love's garden are subtly and erotically revealed. The count thinks he has caught his wife with Figaro (actually it is Susanna disguised), and he proceeds to humiliate her publicly, with no hint of forgiveness. Suddenly the real countess emerges, and the haughty count must beg her pardon. A pause, and then the countess sings, "I'm more merciful, I say yes." All you need is love: love of the deepest and broadest kind.

By the first rehearsal Mozart knew his opera would be a hit. At the end of the first act the Italian singers and musicians screamed *"Viva grande Mozart!"* the violinists beating their bows against the music stands. Mozart had coached all the singers, and the tenor remembered "his little animated countenance, when lighted up with the glowing rays of genius—it is as impossible to describe it as it would be to paint sunbeams."

The premiere was a thunderous success; according to the tenor, "at the end of the opera I thought the audience would never stop applauding and calling for Mozart." Almost every number was encored, and by the next week encores were forbidden at the opera by imperial decree, presumably in the name of public safety and sobriety.

Of the more than forty thousand operas written since the early seventeenth century, *The Marriage of Figaro* is one of the handful to have survived; it is the earliest work in the repertory of almost every opera house. The psychological reality Mozart created through his extraordinary music ensures its life.

Robert Burns's first book of poetry was published in 1786. "The best laid schemes o' mice and men/Gang aft a-gley."

The funny thing about *The Marriage of Figaro* is that despite its initial triumph it ran for only nine performances, and, when the run ended, an opera by one of Mozart's rivals was equally successful. There was only one Imperial Theater in Vienna and there were many opera composers, any of whom could write nice tunes and all of whom could play politics better than the self-assured, somewhat conceited Mozart. If Mozart was unique in creating characters from caricatures (wily servants and heartbroken wives became human beings), who really cared?

When *The Marriage of Figaro* was first produced in London in 1819, it was in a mangled version arranged by Henry Bishop, composer of the song "Home, Sweet Home." Its integrity as a whole piece meant little to Bishop, who found that "the obstacles, alas, that arose in adapting the music were innumerable."

While waiting for his opera to be produced, Mozart wrote three more piano concertos. No. 22 (K. 482) used clarinets in the orchestra for the first time. The other two, no. 23 (K. 488) and no. 24 (K. 491), were written in two weeks and form one of those pairs of works, one basically happy, the other essentially depressed, that Mozart often produced in his last years. Piano Concerto no. 23 is exuberantly close to the music of *Figaro*—like the opera, punctuated with sadness—and no. 24, in a minor key, is tragic and resigned. Beethoven, when he first heard this concerto as a student, turned to a friend and said, "we shall never get any idea like this."

Just before *Figaro* opened, Mozart went to a costume party dressed as a Hindu philosopher, armed with riddles and "fragments from Zoroaster" that he himself had written.

Mozart considered a new tour to improve his fortunes; English friends urged him to go to London. From Salzburg came the news that Leopold would not take care of Mozart's children (Constanze was pregnant again) while the composer and his wife "set out light-heartedly on their travels, die perhaps, perhaps stay in England." So Mozart composed chamber music for sale to amateurs, including two wonderful piano quartets (piano, violin, viola, and cello, K. 478 and K. 493). He had to write to publishers and plead that they take his works (Leopold wrote on his behalf, too), often settling for a ridiculously small fee; twenty years later, the same publishers begged Beethoven for scores. The Viennese middle classes could support a free-lance composer in 1805, but they were neither rich nor influential enough in 1785. If Mozart had lived just a little longer his financial success would have been substantial.

At his Masonic lodge, Mozart met Anton Stadler, a virtuoso on Mozart's beloved clarinet. The first work he wrote for him, a Trio for Clarinet, Viola, and Piano (K. 498), combines Mozart's three favorite solo instruments and is hypnotically lovely.

In October 1786 the Mozart's third child was born. Constanze became seriously ill, and the boy died that November.

For his December concerts, Mozart composed two of his most seductive and expressive orchestral works. His Piano Concerto no. 25 (K. 503), the twelfth in two years, is ardent and rich yet totally poised and balanced. The Symphony no. 38 (K. 504) begins with an incredibly beautiful theme even by Mozartean standards. Its romantic melodies become voluptuous, although the quality of yearning is still there. In terms of orchestral sound, it is as glorious as anything Mozart ever wrote.

This symphony is known as the *Prague* Symphony, because of the tremendous reception it received when Mozart performed it there. He and Constanze left for Prague in January 1787 to see a production of *The Marriage of Figaro* which was said to surpass the Viennese one. The opera's success in Prague was unprecedented and unmarred by intrigue: continuous performances, sold-out houses, long lines at the theater, rave reviews (the press did not hesitate to use the word "masterpiece"). And best of all, most of its tunes had been arranged for small ensembles and were played in cafés and beerhalls all over Prague. "Here they talk of nothing but *Figaro*, scrape, blow, whistle, sing nothing but *Figaro*," Mozart wrote. Everywhere he went they were playing his song. Like most composers he wrote to communicate as well as to express his feelings, and he wanted as many people as possible to hear and love his music.

His appearance at the opera house resulted in a near riot; impromptu poems of praise rained down from the galleries. The *Prague* Symphony was played everywhere, always to cheers. These two months in Prague were the zenith of Mozart's personal fame as an adult, and possibly his happiest time since early childhood.

When he left, he carried away the warmest memories, more money than he was used to, and a commission for a new opera for the Prague opera's upcoming fall season.

Mozart went straight to da Ponte, who suggested the story of Don Juan, the archetypal seducer, blasphemer, and egoist. He was already the hero of a number of plays (including one by Moliere), ballets, and operas, and had become practically a legend, like Faust, whose story Goethe was about to begin. The Don Juan story, like any legend, means different things to different people at different times, but always has meaning to everyone. Comic and tragic elements coexist, and the supernatural is pervasive. All this appealed greatly to Mozart, as did his knowledge that an adoring public eagerly awaited it.

Da Ponte worked on the libretto while writing two others. He revealed his inspiration in his memoirs: "I sat down at my writing table with a little bottle of Tokay on my right. . . . A beautiful sixteen-year-old girl was living in my house (I should have wished to love her only as a daugher—but—). She came into my room whenever I rang, which in truth was fairly often." Life imitating art.

As usual, Mozart composed instrumental works while writing his opera. Another pair of emotionally complementary works emerged: two string quintets (second viola was added to the quartet group). They are among the best-loved of all Mozart's chamber music; Quintet no. 3 (K. 515) glows with radiant joy, while Quintet no. 4 (K. 516) breathes anguish and sorrow. He also composed his last serenade, the extremely popular and festive *Eine kleine Nachtmusik* (K. 525). Although the title is easily translatable (*A Little Night Music*, but there's nothing little or nocturnal about the music), its German name has stuck. (A shopper once went to a record store to buy this wonderful music, which she had heard on the radio. When asked what she was looking for, she said "You're not going to believe this, but it's by Mozart and it's called 'I'm Inclined to Knock Music.' ")

In April 1787, Mozart learned that his father was sick. After wishing him a speedy recovery, Mozart shared with him his ideas about death, which had deepened through his contact with Freemasonry. "Since death, when we come to consider it, is seen to be the true goal of life, I have made acquaintance with this best and truest friend of mankind." One of Mozart's close friends had recently died, "just thirty-one years old—my own age. I do not grieve for him—but I do from my heart pity myself." He ended the letter by urging Leopold not to conceal any further deterioration so his "most obedient son," as Mozart still signed himself, could "come with all human speed to your arms." This was Mozart's last letter to Leopold.

Three days later a sullen and poorly dressed young man of sixteen called on Mozart. He had just come from Bonn and was eager to study with the famous composer. Mozart had him improvise—his acid test of musical talent—and detected originality and power; "Keep your eyes on him," Mozart allegedly told a friend. "Some day he will give the world something to talk about." But two weeks later the young Beethoven returned home to take care of his dying mother. He didn't return to Vienna until after Mozart's death.

At the end of May, Mozart received the news that Leopold, then sixty-eight, had died. Nannerl had not told him immediately, and Mozart had no chance to see him for a final time or to attend his funeral. Whatever unresolved bitterness remained between them, Mozart was deeply saddened by his father's death, as streams of memories flooded his brain. For all Leopold's flaws, his infantilizing and criticisms, he had taught, supported, promoted, and idolized his son—at least as a musician—as long as he lived. Later that year Mozart's doctor died at twenty-nine. Both deaths were on his mind when he wrote, "He is at rest! But we shall never be at rest again, until we have the joy of seeing him again in a better world, and never more to part."

Mozart's relationship with his sister ceased soon after Leopold's death. After her brother died, Nannerl supplied copious details about Mozart's life to his first biographer. For events after 1781, she curtly wrote, "you must make enquiries in Vienna."

In October 1787, Mozart and Constanze, who was again pregnant, returned to Prague for the production of his new opera, then almost finished. As usual the overture was written last, two nights before the first performance. Constanze remembered keeping her sleepy husband calm and awake by filling him with punch and telling him smutty stories of the sort he liked so well.

Rehearsals were difficult, because the work Mozart presented was exceedingly complex and full of problems in singing, playing, and staging. Rumor spread that, in the interests of realism, Mozart was having affairs with all three sopranos; he is known to have rushed up behind one of them and scared her into producing the kind of realistic scream she had been unwilling to attempt. Added accuracy may have come from Casanova, a friend of da Ponte's then staying in Prague, who looked over the libretto.

Don Giovanni (K. 527), subtitled "The Rake Punished," was first performed at the end of October 1787. The central character, a dissolute aristocrat, begins the opera by attempting to rape Donna Anna, a friend of his; he is masked and not

Scene from Don Giovanni *(New York City Opera): The confident Giovanni toasts his masked guests.*

recognized, nor is it clear how far he has gotten with her. Within minutes Giovanni has killed her aged father, the commendatore, who has come to his daughter's defense. Donna Anna and her fiancé, the well-meaning but simpering Don Ottavio, swear revenge.

Giovanni couldn't care less—he's seen a new potential conquest. She turns out to be Donna Elvira, whom he had seduced and abandoned some time before. Extremely high-strung, Elvira threatens to "cut out his heart" if he won't marry her. Giovanni laughingly gives her the slip, leaving his servant, Leporello, to remind her she is "neither the first nor the last." While singing an aria detailing his master's conquests, he unfolds an increasingly long list, a catalogue of types Giovanni has had around the world; "in Spain alone," Leporello sings, "one thousand and three."

Giovanni next interrupts the wedding festivities of two peasants, diverting the groom, Masetto, and coming on to the lovely Zerlina. His passionate wooing wins her over, but Elvira comes by and denounces him. Anna and Ottavio enter, and in the wonderful quartet which follows, Anna recognizes her father's murderer. Giovanni quickly leaves. Elvira, Anna, and Ottavio, in masks, attend a gala party at Giovanni's where the host attempts to rape Zerlina (it's her off-stage scream that Mozart coached). The three unmask and attack Giovanni, but amid thunder and lightning he laughingly escapes, ending the first act.

By the end of act 1, Giovanni, who in the first ten minutes is shown to be a pitiless murderer and rapist, has become the hero. The other characters, like the audience, are extremely ambivalent about him; they condemn his deeds but admire his energy, sexuality, charm, and complete independence. He is a force, a law unto himself. All the women in the opera are as captivated by him as they are repelled, and though they constantly swear vengeance, each in her own way is in love with him.

The second act is as passionate and violent as the first, though the opera is as a whole some kind of comedy. Giovanni and Leporello exchange clothes, deluding the gullible Elvira into embracing the servant. (Switched identities occur in all Mozart's late operas.) Giovanni easily outwits his opponents, leaving Leporello to take a beating at their hands.

Then the supernatural enters: Giovanni and Leporello are hiding in a cemetery and notice a statue of the late commendatore. Giovanni forces his trembling servant to invite the statue to dinner; the statue first nods, then sings "Yes." Leporello is horrified, but Giovanni smirks. The dead don't frighten him any more than the living, and nothing is sacred. He grows increasingly attractive.

The last scene is a dinner party. On-stage musicians play snatches of various popular operas, including *The Marriage of Figaro*. Elvira rushes in, falls on her knees, and begs Giovanni to repent. Mockingly he sinks to his knees beside her, remorseless. She runs out and screams: in walks the statue. It's not interested in food, the statue assures his host, but invites Giovanni to dine with him. Only momentarily nonplussed, Giovanni gives his hand in assent.

The music becomes darker, more frightening. The statue's hand won't let go. "Repent!" shouts the statue, as the music thunders out the chilling ascending and descending chromatic scales first heard in the overtures; the notes go up and down the spine. "No," Giovanni sneers, refusing to repent, give in, conform. Flames leap out and the statue leads the still-defiant Giovanni into hell. The damned don't cry.

The first-night audience was astonished: the boldness of Giovanni's character and the vividness of the music, the richness of characterization of nobility, servants, and peasants. The total effect is beyond romantic, practically expressionistic. The music underlines the ambiguities, the conflicting emotions, the personality differences of the protagonists; popular tunes meet formal arias, and the instrumental music has enormous power.

Reactions were mixed, but mostly favorable. "Connoisseurs and musicians say that Prague has never yet heard the like" wrote one reviewer, and it was exactly the newness of the experience that made immediate rapture difficult. The opera was repeated and was definitely a success, but nothing like that of *Figaro*.

In the eighteenth century, *Don Giovanni* was at first condemned because of its story, which John Ruskin called "the most monstrous of conceivable subjects." But to others it was a colossus that dwarfed everything in its path, the first presentation of what was later called the Superman, the individual beyond society or morality. Superlatives never before used were employed to describe its overwhelming force. Even Wagner, never generous in praise of others' music, wrote, "Is it possible to find anything more perfect than every piece of *Don Giovanni?*" There's no sense in calling any one work Mozart's greatest, but one can have favorites; for many people *Don Giovanni* is the one work they would take to that desert island.

Mozart was tempted to stay in Prague, but two events made him return to Vienna. Constanze was eight months pregnant and wanted to give birth at home, and Mozart learned that Gluck, who held the post of imperial court composer, had died. Mozart saw no reason why he should not be appointed to the post, especially after his operatic successes. He was full of hopes when he returned to Vienna in November 1787; he seemed at the threshold of his greatest success. He was still young, at the height of his powers, famous and happy and productive.

He was also restless, nervous, significantly in debt, in poor health, and full of premonitions. He had only four more years to live.

6.

Midnight Sun

Even my work gives me no pleasure.
—Mozart, 1791

As soon as he returned home, Mozart's direst fears seemed justified. He was indeed appointed Gluck's successor, but at less than half his salary. Mozart earned eight hundred gulden a year and received about five hundred per opera. When Emperor Joseph's youngest daughter came of age, the emperor gave her a birthday present of ninety thousand gulden.

The Mozarts' first daughter was born in December. She died a few months later.

At the end of December, Haydn refused an opera commission from Prague "since the great Mozart can scarcely have his equal." He advised the Praguers to retain Mozart and pay him well, "for without that the story of great genius is a sad one and gives posterity little encouragement for further effort; for which reason, alas, so many hopeful spirits suffer defeat."

As imperial court composer, Mozart's main job was to provide dance music for royal balls, which he did, often using tunes from his operas. His official obligations cut into his concert schedule, and he wrote only one new work, the Piano Concerto no. 26 (K. 537), for his own use. His childhood seriousness about music extended to his performances: whether at home or on stage, he immediately stopped playing if anyone made the slightest noise.

He spent much time in early 1788 preparing for the Vienna premiere of *Don Giovanni*. Except for his sister-in-law Aloysia Lange, who sang Donna Anna, and the baritone who sang the title role, each singer was dissatisfied with his or her part. Mozart wrote a new tenor aria because the singer found the original one too difficult; both are so beautiful that each has been retained, one in each act. His rivals were actively campaigning against him, too; among their grudges was that Mozart, at singers' requests, wrote arias for them to insert in other composers' operas, and his work often put the rest of the music to shame. And as in any sophisticated city, there were people who were tired of hearing about Mozart's triumphs and would be amused to see him fall.

Don Giovanni opened in Vienna in April 1788. It was a failure.

No work in the history of music, no matter how extraordinary, has ever been greeted with unanimous praise: Beethoven's Ninth Symphony, Tchaikovsky's Violin Concerto, and Brahms's Fourth Symphony were panned by respected critics, and Clara Schumann thought that the prelude to Wagner's *Tristan and Isolde* was the ugliest thing she'd ever heard. Still, it is difficult to imagine how *Don Giovanni* could have flopped in Vienna. It was too long, critics said, full of excesses, chromatic and dissonant, tortured, too funny, not funny enough. The ever astute emperor remarked that Mozart's music was "certainly too difficult for the singers," and although "the music is divine, even more beautiful than *Figaro,* such music is not for the teeth of my Viennese." After fifteen performances the opera was dropped and not revived in Mozart's lifetime. Haydn refused to join in the fashionable attack, stating "all I know is that Mozart is the greatest living composer."

In 1788, Gibbons published *The Decline and Fall of the Roman Empire,* a study of the "vicissitudes of fortune which spares neither man nor the proudest of his works, which buries empires and cities in a common grave."

Mozart changed that summer. The failure of *Don Giovanni* made the shallowness and capriciousness of Viennese society painfully clear. Constanze was sick, and medicine was expensive. Fewer and fewer people subscribed to his concerts, ordered his scores (for which publishers paid less and less), or even appeared for lessons. Anxious about money, he wrote to Michael Puchberg, a banker and brother Mason: "I will go straight to the point. If you could be so kind, so friendly, as to lend me one or two thousand gulden." Later that month a second letter announced, "I cannot possibly pay you back so soon." The letters to Puchberg continued uninterrupted, always asking for more money, sometimes as little as twenty-five gulden.

The Mozarts had moved several times, generally to smaller or more suburban locations. Now Mozart had a small garden to compose in, and to try to dispel the increasing periods of depression.

In the midst of his many worries, Mozart performed a remarkable feat: in six weeks of nonstop work from June to August he composed his last three symphonies, no. 39 (K. 543), no. 40 (K. 550), and no. 41 (K. 551), called the *Jupiter* Symphony. (Like most musical nicknames, this one was invented by later critics, and it had nothing to do with Mozart's thoughts. Someone tried to attach the name *Venus* to Symphony no. 40, but fortunately it didn't stick. Who knows how long Piano Concerto no. 21 will be known as the *Elvira Madigan?*)

These symphonies were never heard in Mozart's lifetime. He didn't write them for a concert or a patron; he just seemed to have three symphonies in his head and wanted to get them out, whether he heard them played or not. Once written he could hear them the way the deaf Beethoven could "hear" his Ninth Symphony. No sketches exist for these works: they apparently developed complete in Mozart's imagination, including the great five-part fugue that closes the *Jupiter* Symphony. Each is different and distinct. Symphony no. 39 has a ripe, rich sound, and it ends with a fanfare that abruptly stops in the middle of a phrase. The two others form a characteristic Mozartean pair; the minor-key no. 40 is anguished and sad, the *Jupiter* Symphony triumphant and proud. These descriptions are merely crude suggestions, because the music of all three is infinitely expressive and multileveled. Shortly after Mozart's death, his last three symphonies became among his most frequently performed works. There have been bigger and grander symphonies, but none better. However fatalistic Mozart had become, he could still express his affirmation of life in music.

Mozart dedicated his next work to Puchberg, who no doubt would have preferred some of his money back. The Divertimento for String Trio (K. 563) combines the light, popular form of the serenade with fugal and other formal elements of three-part string writing. Because it is such a perfect synthesis of these two major aspects of Mozart's art, some people find it a distillation — essence of Mozart.

At the end of the year Mozart's old friend van Swieten came to his aid. Van Swieten was still interested in "old" music, and he paid Mozart to update some of Handel's oratorios to suit contemporary taste: harmonic alterations, some streamlining, reorchestration. Mozart's version of *Messiah* was used throughout the nineteenth and early twentieth centuries, and only since the 1950s have Handel's major works been performed more or less as he wrote them.

The revolutionary new year, 1789, changed Europe and the world forever. Mozart composed very little, except more court dances. Of his low salary he remarked, "Too much for what I do, too little for what I could do." His pains and melancholy increased. He may have had a kidney disease that gradually weakened him in body and spirit.

A Danish visitor noticed that "everything that surrounded this splendid man was musical." Mozart, restless and distracted, played piano constantly, Constanze and little Karl singing. Unlike Leopold, Mozart tended to his son's musical education rather casually.

Friends were thoughtful enough to send Mozart clippings from newspapers and music journals. Of his operas, *Idomeneo* was never performed, *The Abduction from the Seraglio* played all over Europe, but to mixed reviews, the most frequent complaint being that its "strange harmonies" were unsuited to the theater; and as for *Figaro*, which was performed in both Italian and German, that "silly piece" had "outlived its term." His music was thought to be exaggerated, overly passionate, too complex — not "classical," but defiantly "modern." "He gives his hearers no time to breathe," complained one critic who might better have been grateful. "As soon as one beautiful melody is grasped, it is succeeded by another." A journalist bemoaned Mozart's "overloaded orchestra."

Mozart was not long dead before his same compositions were used as models of clarity and restraint with which to attack the "romantic" music of his successors, Beethoven and Schubert.

This unfinished portrait of Mozart at age 33, painted by the composer's brother-in-law, is said to be the closest likeness of him.

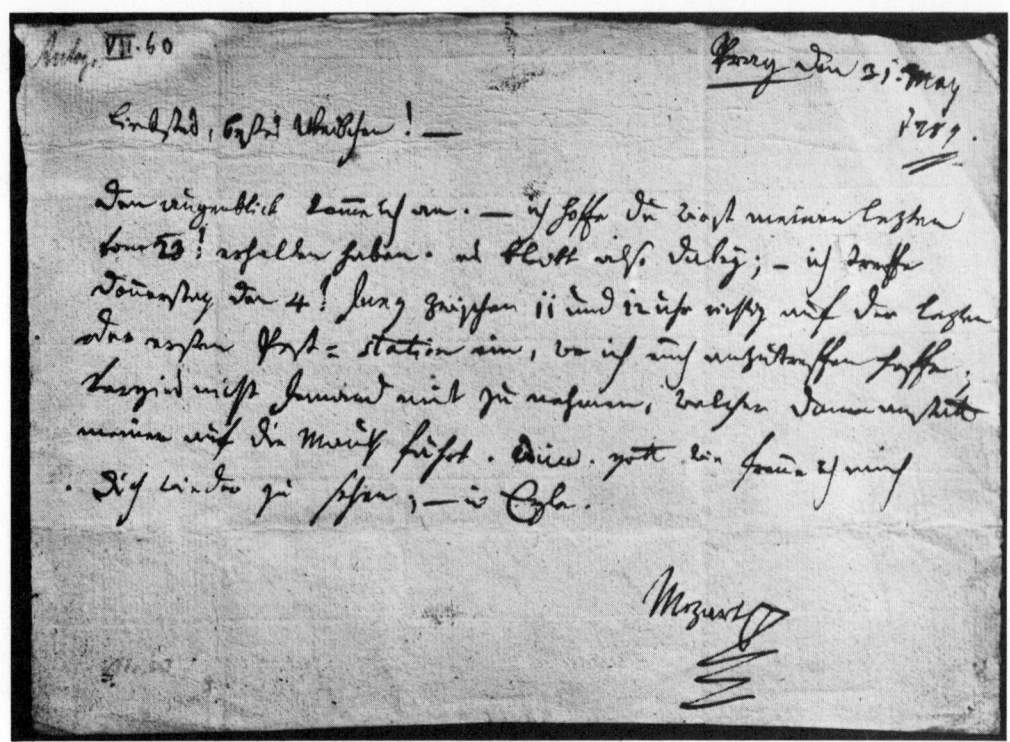
A letter from Mozart to Constanze.

Storming the Bastille, Paris, July 14, 1789.

In April 1789, Mozart gladly accepted an invitation from an aristocratic pupil to accompany him on a trip to the Prussian capital, Berlin. Travel always excited Mozart, and his concerts along the way in Dresden and Leipzig attracted enthusiastic crowds. In Leipzig he visited Saint Thomas's Church, where Johann Sebastian Bach had spent his last years. Mozart played the same organ Bach had played for twenty-five years. Bach's former pupil and successor, the seventy-four-year-old Johann Doles, thought his late master had come back in Mozart. Doles was surprised in the interest so modern a composer took in Bach's neglected works, and in Mozart's honor Doles led the chorus in a Bach motet for eight-part double chorus. An observer wrote that as Mozart listened "his whole soul seemed to be in his ears."

The face of one great composer as he heard the music of another: more than a century later Alma Mahler watched from backstage as her husband conducted the "Love-Death" from Wagner's *Tristan*. "The sight of his face, uplifted and open-mouthed, was so inexpressibly moving that I felt a thrill of utter conviction: I knew once and for all it was my mission in life to live for him alone." Gustav Mahler and Richard Strauss, both conductors as well as composers, led a great Mozart revival in the early 1900s, playing orchestral works which had seldom been heard and supervising strong, insightful productions of his operas. Alma Mahler recorded her husband's last moments as he lay dying in Vienna in 1911. "Mahler lay there with dazed eyes; one finger was conducting on the quilt. There was a smile on his lips and twice he said: 'Mozart!'"

The Prussian king, a cellist and music lover, welcomed Mozart and commissioned some string quartets and a few sonatas; nothing more. On his way back, Mozart again went to Leipzig, where he achieved such orchestral volume at a concert that people feared the old building would collapse. But the monetary gain was slight; as he wrote to his wife, "you must rejoice more at having me home again than any money I bring." He was back in Vienna by June 1789.

Needless to say Constanze was pregnant, and sick besides. She began a series of cures at a fashionable spa outside Vienna. Mozart turned to Puchberg: "God! I am in a situation I wouldn't wish on my worst enemy. . . . O God! instead of thanks, I have only new pleas for you!"

Two days after Mozart wrote this letter, an enraged crowd of Parisians stormed and liberated the hated Bastille prison, symbol of feudal repression. The armed phase of the French Revolution had begun.

At first, life in Vienna continued as usual. In August *The Marriage of Figaro* was revived, despite its connections to the French Revolution, in which servants were really outsmarting their masters (feudalism was abolished in France that same month). The emperor commissioned another opera from Mozart and da Ponte. The poet decided to be original, and he based his libretto on an anecdote told to him by the gossipy emperor. It, too, concerns love, disguises, ideals, and character.

The Mozarts' fifth child, a girl, was born in November 1789 and died after an hour.

Love must have been on Mozart's mind when he composed a Quintet for Clarinet and Strings (K. 581), also for Stadler. Mozart's use of the clarinet in his last years was echoed by Brahms, who also was inspired by a specific instrumentalist. When he was twenty-three, the struggling, self-critical Brahms wrote, "How lucky is the man who, like Mozart and others, goes to the tavern of an evening and writes some fresh music. For he lives while he is creating, though he does what he likes."

Mozart thought a lot about love while Constanze was away at the spa. "I am glad indeed when you have some fun—of course I am—but I do wish that you would sometimes not make yourself so cheap," wrote the jealous husband. Insecurity in matters of love was part of Mozart's basic makeup.

Fidelity is the theme of *Così fan tutte (That's What All Women Do,* K. 588). Two young officers, Ferrando and Guglielmo, are goaded by their cynical friend Don Alfonso to bet on the faithfulness of their lovers, two extravagantly affectionate sisters named Dorabella and Fiordiligi. The men announce they must go to war, and after a tearful farewell they return, disguised as Albanians, and attempt to seduce each other's lover. They are aided by the sisters' maid, Despina, whose no-nonsense view of men is that "one is as good as the other because none is worth anything," and who firmly believes women should love for "convenience and vanity."

At first the two couples are undifferentiated, but gradually their differences emerge. Ferrando is reluctant to pursue his quarry, while Guglielmo begins to enjoy his role. And Dorabella impulsively succumbs without much effort while Fiordiligi resists heroically—but she, too, gives in at last. The men remove their disguises and the original couples reunite, wiser about love, themselves, each other. It's all right that the women aren't goddesses.

A bauble about four people with nothing better to do with their time than play games; yet the music makes it much more. It may be Mozart's most beautiful opera (although any one could be, usually the one most recently heard). The music is shimmering, iridescent; ravishing melodies for an opera about seduction. What makes this work an emotionally compelling experience is the interplay of satire and genuine feeling. Each character is exaggerated, and foolish attitudes are ridiculed, but Mozart's heart is with his lovers, not coldly above them. The music illuminates love's many sides: the blissful intoxication of sexual love, the sorrow of parting, the self-doubts, jealousies, and insecurities, the way one's feelings can suddenly change despite one's best intentions. As the men leave, the women sing, "Write to me every day" and "Stay faithful." Their blending voices are the real thing: there's no more joke, no more opera, just the memory of a lover's leaving and the fear of being forgotten or replaced. "How everything can change in a minute," the women sing later.

The heart of the opera is Fiordiligi's capitulation. Everyone around her urges her to give in, but she decides on a dramatic move: she'll join her man at the front. She sits down, takes off her wig, but, before she can change clothes, in walks Ferrando. Their duet grows more and more passionate until Fiordiligi meltingly yields to Ferrando; he, like the audience, both regrets her fall from resolve and admires the fullness of her ardor. The world of love, where, as Hippolyte Taine wrote, "the air is so soft that one has only to breathe it to be happy."

Così fan tutte's frankness, humor, and sexual sophistication delighted the first-night audience in January 1790. But by nineteenth-century standards it was "immoral"; Beehoven and Wagner denounced it. Chunks of its beautiful music were performed to other plays and even to religious texts. It is probably the least often heard of Mozart's late operas; it was not performed at the Metropolitan Opera until 1922.

Fate again worked against Mozart. Whatever success *Così fan tutte* might have had was cut short by Emperor Joseph's death and the closing of the opera in mourning. Although Joseph II didn't do nearly enough for Mozart, he was a music lover and to some extent, however ungenerously, a patron. He fancied himself a liberal, and was somewhat sympathetic to Freemasonry, limited religious tolerance, and agrarian reform—although he favored nothing so shockingly radical as abolishing serfdom. His successor and younger brother, Leopold II, was another story: a total reactionary who cared little for music. Of course the world was different, changed in a moment: the French Revolution's progress made aristocrats all over Europe angry and afraid. Like his predecesssor, Leopold II was Marie Antoinette's brother.

Outwardly, politics did not interest Mozart. But in the larger sense of the word—how people treat each other—Mozart's politics stressed the brotherhood of man, hatred of injustice and abuse, and love of liberty.

Mozart was sick most of that summer. His application for a raise was turned down, and he was not invited to play or compose for the emperor's forthcoming coronation as Holy Roman Emperor in Frankfurt. Mozart was not even asked to attend. Pawning some few remaining valuables—all those pocket watches—Mozart set off for Frankfurt anyway, to take advantage of the large crowds. His wife, sick again, remained in Vienna.

His concerts in Frankfurt and neighboring cities were only moderately successful. He played his Piano Concerto no. 26 of two years back during the festivities, and it subsequently acquired the name *Coronation* Concerto; it was Mozart's most famous for the next hundred years. He was depressed and lonely; he wrote to his "dearest, best little wife of my heart" that "tears rained upon the paper as I wrote." But his love for her cheered him: "Catch! An astonishing number of kisses are flying about." He returned home in November after two months on the road. He did not stop in his hated Salzburg or visit his sister.

His friends noticed a marked physical decline. Although he had been pale for most of his life, he was now practically white, and his blue eyes bulged: possibly a result of kidney failure. His bushy blond hair, "of which he was rather vain," was thinning.

Haydn came to say goodbye to Mozart at the end of the year. He was on his way to London, fame, and fortune, and he urged Mozart to come with him. Mozart refused: too ill, exhausted, Constanze pregnant, not up for travel. Mozart wept bitterly when Haydn left, believing rightly that he would never again see his beloved friend, who so consistently praised and appreciated him. "I am not the best of my school, though I was the first," the modest Haydn later wrote.

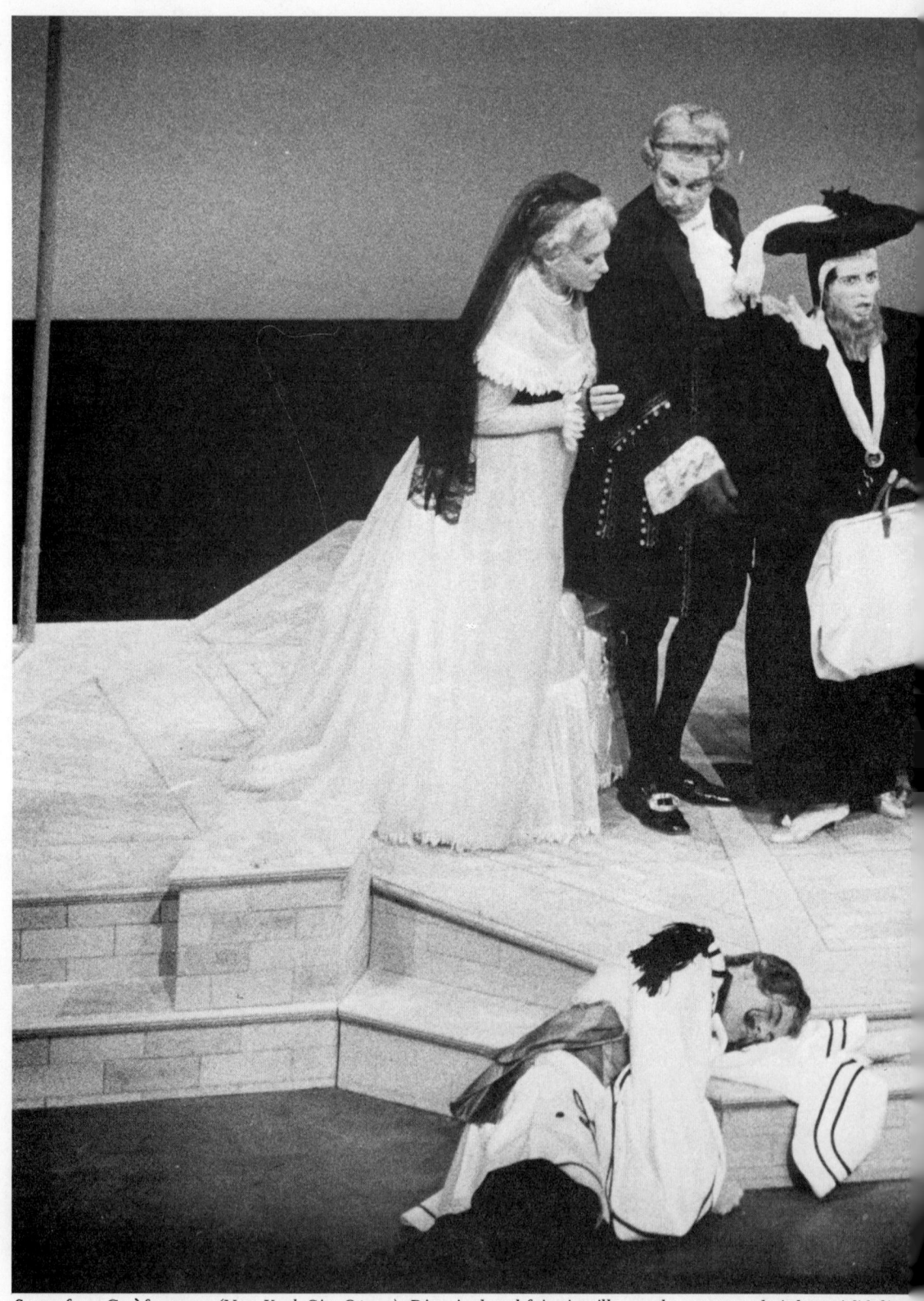
Scene from Così fan tutte *(New York City Opera): Disguised and feigning illness, the men test their lovers' fidelity.*

The winter of 1790–1791 was unusually cold in Vienna, and a visitor to the Mozarts' apartment found the couple dancing away madly; they were keeping warm, Mozart laughed, since they could not afford firewood. But his cheerfulness increasingly gave way to despondency. If he were suffering from kidney disease, his body was poisoning itself, leaving him drained and depressed. At that time diagnosis was so primitive and treatment so harmful (bloodletting was still the first thing tried) that it didn't much matter that Mozart had only the scantest medical attention.

Everything that Mozart composed in 1791 is colored, to a listener who knows, by its being his last year alive, a fact Mozart may have suspected but could not have known until winter. For an anonymous Hungarian music lover he wrote his last two string quintets, no. 5 (K. 593) and no. 6 (K. 614), both reflective and inward pieces with fugal finales. He wrote small pieces for two novelty instruments: a "mechanical organ," a small organ placed inside a clock and operated by the clockwork mechanism, and "glass harmonica," a series of water-filled bowls spun on a treadle, squeaking out a sound by the friction of finger on wet glass.

Mozart had not given an all-Mozart concert in Vienna for years; in March, he performed at a benefit for a clarinetist. For this, his last public concert, he wrote his last piano concerto, no. 27 (K. 595). The sound is leaner, simpler, more personal than the earlier concertos, which were written for a bravura pianist constantly concertizing. A favorite of Brahms's, the Piano Concerto no. 27 shares with much of that composer's music the quality described as autumnal.

Yet the paradox of eternal youth remained: Mozart was still young, still enjoyed practical jokes, nonsense stories, and dirty ditties (some of which he set to the music of his piano sonatas), and, however full of resignation his music became, it never lost a sense of perpetual freshness. Life does go on.

Much of Mozart's gloominess was dispelled in March, when a new opera commission arrived from Schikaneder, his old Salzburg actor friend now living in Vienna. Schikaneder had taken over a large suburban theater, in which he presented entertainment for the masses: pantomimes, farces, variety acts of all kinds. A Freemason, Schikaneder had written a confused patchwork story, part fairy tale, part slapstick, and part serious philosophical speculation and political metaphor, that he wanted Mozart to set to music. Mozart decided to do a real opera, incorporating all aspects of the play in appropriate musical styles. It would be in German with spoken dialogue, and it would attract a different audience than the snobbish crowd at the Imperial Opera. Mozart was familiar with inconsistency: as he worked with pleasure on his first German opera in ten years, his joy alternated with sickness, money problems, and sleepless nights.

He was interrupted more than once. In June, sick and inevitably pregnant, Constanze left for the spa. Mozart visited her there and composed a small piece of church music, the hymn *Ave, verum corpus* (K. 618) for four voices, organ, and strings. Like his Masonic music, it has a distinctly otherworldly sound. Did he know? It is music, as Eric Blom wrote, that has "the unearthly quality one cannot imagine to have come from any human being but one facing extinction."

Mozart, age 35.

Emanuel Schikaneder.

In July, Mozart wrote to his wife, "I cannot describe what I have been feeling—a kind of emptiness, which hurts me dreadfully—a kind of longing, which is never satisfied."

Constanze returned at the end of the month, and the Mozarts' sixth child was born. Franz Xaver Wolfgang survived. He studied music and became a pianist and composer, not surprisingly calling himself Wolfgang Mozart, Jr. His music doesn't have the faintest glimmer of his father's genius. Like his brother Karl he became rich from his father's estate, and he, too, was unmarried when he died, in 1844.

Mozart's German opera was almost finished when a new commission literally materialized. A tall stranger dressed in gray came to Mozart's house. He wanted a requiem, a mass for the dead. He'd pay well, and half in advance, but there was one condition: the requiem was to remain a secret, its patron mysterious. Mozart agreed.

He began working on it immediately. The request and its delivery startled him, and in his feverish and exhausted state he half-believed that the stranger had been a messenger announcing Mozart's imminent death. He became convinced he was writing his own requiem.

Mozart's sons: Franz Xaver and Karl.

Scene from The Magic Flute *(New York City Opera): Beverly Sills as the Queen of the Night.*

In fact the mystery man was the steward of Count von Walsegg, a musical amateur who, like many others, paid composers to write music which he passed off as his own. His wife had just died and he wanted to honor her memory with a requiem; the solemnity of the occasion didn't prevent Walsegg's self-aggrandizing fraud.

A third commission bumped both opera and mass. Among Emperor Leopold II's titles was king of Bohemia, and he was going to be crowned in Prague in September. (His many coronations seem particularly ludicrous since he died the following March.) He gave Mozart a text to set as a serious opera, a form Mozart had not used since *Idomeneo*. Though uninterested in the stale plot and disinclined to travel, Mozart could not refuse. He left for Prague at the end of August with Constanze and one of his few remaining pupils, Franz Süssmayr. The gray-coated stranger approached Mozart just as he entered the coach and asked how the requiem was coming—a fine way to start the trip.

The opera was scheduled for production in two weeks. Mozart wrote in the carriage and late into the night at inns, supplying the last touches just hours before the performance. Süssmayr wrote the recitatives, and Mozart the arias and ensembles.

Titus's Clemency (K. 621) is stiff, formal, and has none of the psychological penetration of his other late operas. It does contain some especially romantic, chromatic melodies, lush and sensual scoring, and a wonderful ensemble depicting a fire, riot, and assassination attempt at the Roman Capitol. It was not a success, and the new empress called it "German piggery." Its lovely tunes and sentimental morality made it Mozart's most popular opera for much of the nineteenth century (Shelley wrote a poem inspired by it), and it is certainly worth hearing despite its weaknesses.

His German opera was ready in September, and he conducted the premiere of *The Magic Flute* (K. 620) himself. Tamino, a young Oriental prince, is approached by the Queen of the Night. She shows him a portrait of her daughter, Pamina, who has been kidnapped by an evil magician, Sarastro. If Tamino can free her he can have her. To assist him she lends him her bird catcher, Papageno, sort of a large bird himself, covered with feathers. She also gives him a magic flute, and Papageno gets a magic glockenspiel.

But when they reach Sarastro's palace they find that it is the Temple of Reason, Nature, and Wisdom. Sarastro has indeed taken Pamina, but to save her from her wicked mother. Sarastro tests Tamino to see if he can become a member of the temple. Though some of the stunts seem foolish, they involve the Masonic ideals of triumphing over hate, selfishnesss, and fear of death. Papageno imitates these trials for laughs, even indulging in a comic suicide attempt after a serious one by Pamina, who mistakes Tamino's vow of silence for indifference. The Queen of the Night returns to destroy the temple, but she is defeated and crushed. Tamino gets Pamina, Papageno gets a bird-woman, Papagena, and all live happily in the temple's hallowed halls.

Mozart's music is the most varied imaginable. The Queen of the Night sings icy coloratura, more extreme than any found in Italian opera. Papageno sings popular tunes and waltzes. Sarastro and his priests have Masonic music, rich, deep, moving; Bernard Shaw called it music that could have come out of God's mouth. The contrast is greatest in the second act, when the Queen of the Night tries to force her daughter to kill Sarastro. This "vengeance aria" is fast, hard, cold, and frightening, with leaps and swoops up to the highest top note in opera. Immediately afterward, Sarastro sings of peace and forgiveness; his aria, "In These Hallowed Halls," is slow, pliant, warm, and comforting, gently descending to the lowest note in the bass's range. Love, as always, triumphs.

The Magic Flute was a huge hit. Schikaneder played Papageno, improvising like mad, and Constanze's oldest sister, Josepha Hofer, portrayed the Queen of the Night. Audiences cheered night after night, but Mozart appreciated even more what he called "the silent applause." Schikaneder made a fortune on the initial run alone.

That same September, Mozart wrote his last orchestral work, a Clarinet Concerto (K. 622) for Stadler. Its heartbreaking slow movement is so expressive that it seems that a voice, not a clarinet, is singing low, the words just below the threshold of comprehensibility.

Constanze returned to Vienna from the spa and found Mozart much sicker. She tried to calm him and make him rest, but he insisted on finishing his requiem. Some days he could work, other days he would try but collapse. He felt as if he were being poisoned—it may well have been uremic poisoning; later a rumor spread that Salieri, his rival, had poisoned him. Actually Salieri had been Mozart's guest at *The Magic Flute* and praised it lavishly. But the story spread, Pushkin writing a poem based on the tale. Salieri, who died in 1825, spent his last years insane, incessantly denying that he had poisoned Mozart.

On good days Mozart would visit the theater where *The Magic Flute* was regularly packing them in. He played a practical joke on Schikaneder, who as Papageno pretended to play his glockenspiel. Mozart took over from the off-stage bell-player and deliberately played out of time with Schikaneder, who finally screamed "Shut up!" into the wings. The audience roared; Mozart smiled sweetly.

Ingmar Bergman filmed a Swedish production of *The Magic Flute* which vividly captures, among other aspects, the great fun it must be to perform it.

On bad days Mozart stayed in bed, weak and in pain. He followed the progress of *The Magic Flute* by looking at his watch and singing the music that was being played at the theater just down the street.

He recovered a little in November. He wrote a brief cantata for his Masonic lodge; it ends with the words, "Brothers, join your hands in union." In the middle of the month he conducted it, his last public appearance.

Mozart worked on his requiem whenever he could, and gave Süssmayr oral and written instructions on how to complete it. Though finished by another, the Requiem (K. 626) is unquestionably Mozart's work. One of its themes is taken from Handel's *Messiah,* and some sections are audibly inferior to others. But at its best, as in the Lacrimosa, it is as emotionally intense as were the circumstances surrounding its composition.

In November 1963, Mozart's Requiem was performed at John F. Kennedy's funeral and transmitted by satellite around the world.

On the evening of December 4, 1791, some of Mozart's family and friends were singing the Requiem for Mozart, who was too sick to play it at the piano. When they reached the Lacrimosa, still unfinished, Mozart began to sob. He rapidly became paralyzed. A priest was sent for, and he arrived reluctantly, not knowing the composer, to administer last rites. In his delirium Mozart kept blowing air out of his cheeks, as if playing the Requiem's mighty trumpet and trombone parts. At about one o'clock the next morning, two months before his thirty-sixth birthday, Mozart died.

The exact cause of his death has never been ascertained, despite much research. At one time he was said to have burned himself out; modern science suggests uremic poisoning, rheumatic fever, or some combination.

The room where Mozart died.

Constanze Mozart broke down. Van Swieten arranged the funeral, the cheapest possible one that still afforded any dignity. Mozart was buried with twenty other corpses in an unmarked common grave, but funeral services were held. In addition to saving money, the funeral avoided the ostentation and superstition that Mozart loathed.

Only three mourners appeared at the church: van Swieten, Süssmayr, and Salieri. None of them accompanied the body to the cemetery, presumably because of bad weather.

Thirty-six years later, after a performance of Mozart's Requiem, twenty thousand Viennese followed Beethoven's corpse to its final resting place.

Almost immediately after Mozart's death, his music began to receive the worldwide attention it had so long deserved. Constanze, as the Widow Mozart, organized a series of all-Mozart concerts to benefit herself and her two children. Mozart died owing three thousand gulden—the equivalent of two years' salary plus three operas. The debt was rapidly erased; death had immeasurably enhanced Mozart's reputation and the monetary value of his music.

In 1798, Breitkopf and Härtel, Europe's most prestigious music publisher, announced plans to publish Mozart's complete works. Despite numerous requests from both Leopold and Mozart, the firm had declined to publish any of Mozart's music while he was alive.

Constanze's lot improved too. In 1797 she began living with Georg von Nissen, a Danish diplomat whose love of Mozart's music initially brought them together. A shrewd businessman, Nissen handled negotiations with music publishers, often holding back manuscripts to inflate their price. Following a common practice of the time, Constanze had cut up several of Mozart's scores and used them as calling cards or greeting cards; these were later collected and reassembled. Drawing heavily on Constanze's reminiscences, Nissen wrote the first full-length Mozart biography, which Constanze published in 1828.

One day, while cleaning, Constanze dropped the death mask that had been taken of Mozart. She said "she was glad that the ugly old thing was broken."

Constanze married her lover in 1809, and after a stay in Copenhagen the couple settled in Salzburg. Nannerl Mozart, widowed since 1801, had also moved there, where she earned a living giving piano lessons (many of her pupils became well-known pianists). The two women did not communicate. Nannerl died at seventy-eight in 1829; Constanze was seventy-nine when she died in 1842, more than half a century after her first husband's death.

In the nineteenth century, Mozart's operas, then gradually his instrumental music, became widely known and loved, first among musicians, later by the general public. His music inspired the most extraordinary responses; none is more deeply felt than that of Kierkegaard, who devoted a section of *Either/Or* (1843) to the composer. "Immortal Mozart, you to whom I owe it that I have not gone through this life without being deeply shaken, that I have not died without having loved."

In 1861, on a spot that might have been Mozart's grave, the city of Vienna erected a memorial. It is an ugly Victorian-style column with a weeping angel. As though it were necessary.

Mozart Memorial, Vienna.

Recommended Records

I sensed with all due reverence and modesty that I had gained access to [Mozart's] soul. — Bruno Walter

The record bins under Mozart's name are always bulging. Many Mozart records are very good, but some are special: the result of singers, instrumentalists, and conductors with an affinity for his music. While the clarity of Mozart's music is enhanced by good stereo reproduction and quiet disc surfaces, neither is a substitute for inspiration or commitment.

OPERAS
Idomeneo (K. 366): Glyndebourne Festival Orchestra and Chorus, Pritchard; Seraphim S-6070 (3 records).
The Abduction from the Sergalio (Die Entführung aus dem Serail) (K. 384): Vienna Philharmonic, Krips; Seraphim S-6025 (2 records).
The Marriage of Figaro (Le Nozze di Figaro) (K. 492): Philharmonia Orchestra, Guilini; Angel S-3608 (3 records).
Don Giovanni (K. 527): New Philharmonia Orchestra, Klemperer; Angel S-3700 (4 records).
Così fan tutte (K. 588): Philharmonia Orchestra, Böhm; Angel S-3631 (4 records).
The Magic Flute (Die Zauberflöte) (K. 620): Vienna Philharmonic, Solti; London 1397 (3 records).

SYMPHONIES
Symphonies nos. 25 (K. 183) and 29 (K. 201): Academy of St. Martin-in-the-Fields, Marriner; Argo ZRG-706.
Symphonies nos. 32 (K. 318), 33 (K. 319), and 34 (K. 338): Concertgebouw Orchestra, Krips; Philips 6500526.
Symphonies nos. 35 (*Haffner*, K. 385), 36 (*Linz*, K. 425), 38 (*Prague*, K. 504), 39 (K. 543), 40 (K. 550), and 41 (*Jupiter*, K. 551): Columbia Symphony, Walter; Columbia D3S-691 (3 records).

PIANO CONCERTOS
Concertos nos. 14 (K. 449), 15 (K. 450), 16 (K. 451), 17 (K. 453), 18 (K. 456), and 19 (K. 459): P. Serkin; English Chamber Orchestra, Schneider; RCA ARL3-0732 (3 records).
Concertos nos. 20 (K. 466) and 21 (K. 467): Gulda; Vienna Philharmonic, Abbado; DGG 2530548.
Concertos nos. 23 (K. 488) and 24 (K. 491): Curzon; London Symphony, Kertész; London 6580.
Concertos nos. 25 (K. 503) and 27 (K. 595): De Larrocha; London Philharmonic, Solti; London 7109.
Concerto for Two Pianos (K. 365): H. Menuhin, Fou Ts'ong; Bath Festival Orchestra, Ye. Menuhin; and Concerto for Three Pianos (K. 242): H., Ya., and J. Menuhin; London Philharmonic, Ye. Menuhin; Seraphim S-60072.

OTHER CONCERTOS

Clarinet Concerto (K. 622): Brymer; Academy of St. Martin-in-the-Fields; Marriner; and Bassoon Concerto (K. 191): Chapman; Academy of St. Martin-in-the-Fields, Marriner.

Flute Concerto (K. 313): Monteux; Academy of St. Martin-in-the-Fields, Marriner; and Oboe Concerto (K. 314): Black; Academy of St. Martin-in-the-Fields, Marriner; Philips 6500379.

Flute and Harp Concerto (K. 299): Schulz, Zabaleta; Vienna Philharmonic, Böhm; and *Sinfonia concertante* for Winds (K. App. 9): Vienna Philharmonic; Böhm; DGG 2530715.

Horn Concertos nos. 1 (K. 412), 2 (K. 417), 3 (K. 447), and 4 (K. 495): Tuckwell; London Symphony, Maag; London 6403.

Violin Concertos nos. 1 (K. 207) and 5 (K. 219): Stern; Columbia Symphony, Szell; Columbia MS-6557.

Sinfonia concertante for Violin and Viola (K. 364): Cleveland Orchestra, Szell; Columbia MS-6625.

VOCAL MUSIC

Orphanage Mass (K. 114a): Vienna Philharmonic, Abbado; DGG 2530777.

Exsultate, jubilate (K. 165): Raskin; Cleveland Orchestra, Szell; Columbia MS-6625.

"Great" Mass (K. 427): London Symphony and Chorus, Davis; Philips 6500235.

Requiem (K. 626): Vienna Philharmonic, Böhm; DGG 2530143.

SERENADES

Serenades nos. 6 (K. 239) and 9 ("Posthorn," K. 320): Berlin Philharmonic, Böhm; DGG 2530082.

Serenade no. 7 (*Haffner,* K. 250): Berlin Philharmonic, Böhm; DGG 2530290.

Serenade no. 10 for Winds (K. 361): London Winds, Klemperer; Angel S-36247.

Serenade no. 15 (*Eine kleine Nachtmusik,* K. 525) and Masonic Funeral Music (K. 477): Columbia Symphony, Walter; Odyssey Y-30048.

Divertimento no. 15 (K. 287) and Divertimento for Strings (K. 136): Bath Festival Orchestra, Menuhin; Angel S-36429.

Divertimento no. 17 (K. 334): Academy of St. Martin-in-the-Fields, Marriner; Argo ZRG-705.

CHAMBER MUSIC

String Quartets nos. 14 (K. 387), 15 (K. 421), 16 (K. 428), 17 ("Hunt," K. 458), 18 (K. 464), and 19 ("Dissonance," K. 465) (*Haydn* Quartets): Quartetto Italiano; Philips SC71AX301 (3 records).

String Quintets nos. 1 (K. 174), 2 (K. 406), 3 (K. 515), 4 (K. 516), 5 (K. 593), and 6 (K. 614): Trampler; Budapest Quartet; Columbia D3S-747 (3 records).

Piano Quintet (K. 452): Ashkenazy; London Wind Soloists; London 6494.

String Trio (Divertimento, K. 563): Grumiaux Trio; Philips 802803.

Clarinet Trio (K. 498) and Clarinet Quintet (K. 581): De Peyer; Melos Ensemble; Angel S-36241.

Flute Quartet (K. 285), Oboe Quartet (K. 370), and Horn Quintet (K. 407): Vester, Mater, Bauman; Strauss Quartet; Telefunken 641009.

SONATAS

Piano Sonatas nos. 8 (K. 310), 13 (K. 333), and 14 (K. 457); Fantasy (K. 475): Matthews; Vanguard S-196.

Piano Sonatas nos. 11 (K. 331) and 15 (K. 545); Fantasy (K. 397): Gould; Columbia M-32348.

Sonatas for Two Pianos (K. 448) and Piano Four-Hands (K. 521): Eschenbach and Frantz; DGG 2530285.

Violin Sonatas (K. 296, K. 301, K. 304, K. 376): Druian, Szell; Columbia MS-7064.

Index of Works

Abduction from the Seraglio, The (Die Entführung aus dem Serail) (K. 384), 69, 73-74, 98
Ave, verum corpus (K. 618), 106

Bastien and Bastienne (K. 50), 37-38

Concerto for Bassoon (K. 191), 44
Concerto for Clarinet (K. 622), 50, 111
Concerto for Flute no. 1 (K. 313), 51
Concerto for Flute no. 2 (K. 314), 51
Concerto for Flute and Harp (K. 299), 52
Concerto for Horn no. 1 (K. 412), 77
Concerto for Horn no. 2 (K. 417), 77
Concerto for Horn no. 3 (K. 447), 77
Concerto for Horn no. 4 (K. 495), 77
Concerto for Oboe (K. 314), 51
Concerto for Piano no. 9 (K. 271), 46
Concerto for Piano no. 14 (K. 449), 79
Concerto for Piano no. 15 (K. 450), 79
Concerto for Piano no. 16 (K. 451), 79
Concerto for Piano no. 17 (K. 453), 79
Concerto for Piano no. 18 (K. 456), 79
Concerto for Piano no. 19 (K. 459), 79
Concerto for Piano no. 20 (K. 466), 82
Concerto for Piano no. 21 (K. 467), 82, 97
Concerto for Piano no. 22 (K. 482), 89
Concerto for Piano no. 23 (K. 488), 89
Concerto for Piano no. 24 (K. 491), 89
Concerto for Piano no. 25 (K. 503), 89
Concerto for Piano no. 26 (*Coronation*, K. 537), 96, 103
Concerto for Piano no. 27 (K. 595), 106
Concerto for Two Pianos (K. 365), 56
Concerto for Violin no. 1 (K. 207), 45
Concerto for Violin no. 2 (K. 211), 45
Concerto for Violin no. 3 (K. 216), 45
Concerto for Violin no. 4 (K. 218), 45
Concerto for Violin no. 5 (K. 219), 45
Così fan tutte (K. 588), 52, 102-103, 104-105

Divertimento for Strings (K. 136), 42
Divertimento no. 10 (K. 247), 45
Divertimento no. 11 (K. 251), 45-46
Divertimento no. 15 (K. 287), 45
Don Giovanni (K. 527), 58, 90, 91-95, 96-97

Eine kleine Nachtmusik (K. 525), 90
Exsultate, jubilate (K. 165), 43

Fantasy for Piano (K. 397), 78
Fantasy for Piano (K. 475), 83
Idomeneo (K. 366) 57-59, 63, 73, 98, 110

Magic Flute, The (Die Zauberflöte) (K. 620), 58, 70, 106, 111, 112
Marriage of Figaro, The (Le Nozze di Figaro) (K. 492), 41, 44, 56, 85-89, 90, 94, 95, 98, 101
Masonic Funeral Music (K. 477), 83-84
Mass, *Coronation* (K. 317), 56
Mass, "Great" (K. 427), 77-78
Mass, *Orphanage* (K. 139), 38
Minuet (K. 1), 34

Les petits riens (K. App. 10), 52
Preludes and Fugues (after Bach, K. 404a), 75, 77
Pretended Gardener, The (La finta giardiniera) (K. 196), 44, 47

Quartet for Flute and Strings no. 1 (K. 285), 51
Quartet for Flute and Strings no. 2 (K. App. 171), 51
Quartet for Flute and Strings no. 3 (K. 298), 51
Quartet for Oboe and Strings (K. 370), 59
Quartet for Piano and Strings no. 1 (K. 478), 89
Quartet for Piano and Strings no. 2 (K. 493), 89
Quartet for Strings no. 16 (K. 421), 77, 82
Quartet for Strings no. 17 ("Hunt," K. 458), 79, 82
Quartet for Strings no. 18 (K. 464), 80, 82
Quartet for Strings no. 19 ("Dissonance," K. 465), 80, 82
Quintet for Clarinet and Strings (K. 581), 102
Quintet for Horn and Strings (K. 407), 77
Quintet for Piano and Winds (K. 452), 80

Quintet for Strings no. 3 (K. 515), 90
Quintet for Strings no. 4 (K. 516), 90
Quintet for Strings no. 5 (K. 593), 106
Quintet for Strings no. 6 (K. 614), 106

Requiem (K. 626), 35, 108, 110, 112

Serenade no. 6 ("Serenata notturna," K. 239), 45
Serenade no. 7 (*Haffner*, K. 250), 45
Serenade no. 9 ("Posthorn," K. 320), 56
Serenade no. 10 for Winds (K. 361), 59
Serenade no. 15 (*Eine kleine Nachtmusik*, K. 525), 90
Sinfonia concertante for Violin and Viola (K. 364), 56
Sinfonia concertante for Winds (K. App. 9), 52, 54
Sonata for Piano no. 7 (K. 309), 51
Sonata for Piano no. 8 (K. 310), 55
Sonata for Piano no. 11 (K. 331), 55
Sonata for Piano no. 14 (K. 457), 83
Sonata for Two Pianos (K. 448), 69

Sonatas for Violin and Harpsichord (K. 6-9), 31, 34
Sonata for Violin and Piano (K. 304), 55
Symphony no. 14 (K. 114), 42
Symphony no. 20 (K. 133), 42
Symphony no. 25 (K. 183), 44
Symphony no. 29 (K. 201), 44
Symphony no. 31 (*Paris*, K. 297), 54
Symphony no. 33 (K. 319), 56
Symphony no. 34 (K. 338), 56
Symphony no. 35 (*Haffner*, K. 385), 74-75
Symphony no. 36 (*Linz*, K. 425), 78
Symphony no. 38 (*Prague*, K. 504), 89, 90
Symphony no. 39 (K. 543), 97-98
Symphony no. 40 (K. 550), 97-98
Symphony no. 41 (*Jupiter*, K. 551), 97-98

Titus's Clemency (*La clemenza di Tito*) (K. 621), 110-111
Trio for Clarinet, Viola, and Piano (K. 498), 89
Trio for Strings (Divertimento, K. 563), 98